Treading Lightly with Pack Animals

Treading Lightly
with Pack Animals

A Guide to Low-Impact Travel in the Backcountry

Dan Aadland

Mountain Press Publishing Company
Missoula, Montana
1993

Library of Congress Cataloging-in-Publication Data

Aadland, Dan.
    Treading lightly with pack animals : a guide to low-impact travel in the
        backcountry / Dan Aadland.
            p. cm.
        Includes bibliographical references (p.) and index.
        ISBN 0-87842-297-8 : $15.00
        1. Packhorse camping. 2. Camping—Environmental aspects.
    I. Title.
GV199.7.A33 1993
796.54—dc20   93-39897
                                                                            CIP

Printed in the U.S.A.

MOUNTAIN PRESS PUBLISHING CO.
P.O. Box 2399
Missoula, MT 59806

Treading Lightly with Pack Animals

To Emily, David, Jonathan, and Steve,
partners on the trail.

Treading Lightly with Pack Animals

Table of Contents

Dan Aadland

A teacher and longtime resident of Absarokee, in south-central Montana, Dan Aadland lives just minutes away from some of the most beautiful backcountry the Rocky Mountains have to offer. Dan and his wife, Emily, have taken their family on countless trips into the wilderness, often accompanied by pack animals. Over the years they've managed to learn a few tricks about conservation and preservation, about caring for the land they love, and using pack animals in the most efficient, least destructive methods possible.

In *Treading Lightly with Pack Animals*, Dan blends his love for the outdoors with his expertise in packing and writing. After earning a Ph.D. in English, American Studies, and Creative Writing from the University of Utah in 1973, he launched a career that includes teaching technical and expository writing and free-lance editing. Horses have always figured prominently in Dan's life. He rides 'em, raises 'em, breeds 'em, researches 'em, and reads and writes about 'em. But he's quick to point out that one of the best packing partners he ever had was Smokey, a malamute dog.

Treading Lightly with Pack Animals

Acknowledgments

Special thanks to Tom Simpson for his advice and assistance with the Decker; Robin Smith for his hours of darkroom work; Christie LeClaire Baken and Tom Alt, wilderness rangers of Custer National Forest, for their expert advice on minimal-impact camping; and, as always, to my Number One Editor, Emily, for her help on the manuscript.

Smokey, a malamute pack dog.

Treading Lightly with Pack Animals

Introduction

No one knows just when ancient Man or Woman, sweating under a skin-chafing bundle of belongings, met a donkey or horse or ox on the trail, contemplated its size and strength, then set about finding a way to get the animal to carry a burden. The first attempts were probably clumsy, even comical. But once humans mastered using animals to make their burden lighter, they never looked back. Indeed, from this prehistoric beginning until just a century ago, mankind's animal partners provided the power that made civilization possible.

We've now come full circle. Having created all sorts of machines to transport us and our baggage more swiftly than animals can, we've come to a point of rejecting the mechanical, the noisy, that which smells of exhaust. At least during brief vacation periods, we have come to see the wisdom in Thoreau's dictate that we must simplify life in order to know it better. So we have periodically fled the concrete for a carpet of pine

needles, some of us rejecting all help in carrying the load (though we have enjoyed scientifically designed backpack frames, incredibly convenient stoves, and high-tech foods).

Some of us have answered Thoreau's call strenuously, even passionately. We've rejected the snowmobile in favor of snowshoes, the ski lift for cross-country skis, the motorbike for a good pair of boots. But maybe we've been a bit too hasty in rejecting our first great conveniences: creatures that can subsist on natural foods, that can keep us company, that, if managed properly, do little to damage the environment (perhaps even less than their two-legged companions).

So the cycle is starting on its second revolution. Staring middle age in the face, some of us look at the strength of animals on the trail and think of the things we could take along: thicker sleeping pads (half-inch ensolite just doesn't do it for me any more), better food, and perhaps such previously forbidden luxuries as camp stools. Maybe we've been so dedicated to "health" that jogging has knocked the cartilage from beneath our kneecaps. Maybe in a racketball game we've lost the infamous anterior cruciate ligament. Mine sacrificed itself to an eight-inch pine tree while I was skiing the old-fashioned way, too fast on an icy trail. Like many people, I still can carry a sixty-pound pack down the mountain, but it's not as fun as when my knees were tougher.

So we turn again to ancient Man's wonderful discovery. The seventy-pound German shepherd that cavorts on the trail while you grunt under your pack can contribute to the effort. After an hour or two of training, he won't mind carrying a pack, and into it can go several days' worth of dog food plus assorted items that lighten your own load. A twenty-pound pack for him, if he's healthy and mature, is a lot easier on him than yours is on you.

A pony, llama, or burro can carry packs that would put a grimace on the face of an NFL linebacker, without injury or pain to the animal. An average saddle horse can carry you and your lightweight necessities for an overnight or longer trip, but adding a packhorse (combined with your backpacker's knowledge of weight-saving) can literally set you free for the summer.

So what holds some of us back? Let's be honest. The environmentally conscientious of recent decades have been pretty religious in their zeal, pretty quick to call their own methods pure and those of other folks either unsound or outright harmful. To some of us, full-fledged pack trains with long strings of animals carrying everything but the kitchen sink seem onerous in impact and wasteful.

But travel with animals can be fun, fruitful, and easy on the backcountry. You can engage the help of our animal friends with good conscience. If you've backpacked into pristine country, you have already learned some simple techniques for sparing the environment, and all you need to do now is expand on those. Let's begin this second revolution and rediscover the talents of certain four-footed friends as helpful wilderness companions, as creatures that can take some of the pain out of the backcountry experience. Let's recapture the feeling that comes from cooperating with an animal in a difficult physical task. The cowboy knows that feeling, when he and his horse have taken a hundred cows, single-handedly, across ten miles of open. The dog musher, camped under snowy pines, dogs picketed after a long pull, knows it, too. So does the farmer who, for reasons he can't explain, leaves the tractor in the shed and hitches a team of Belgians to a hay wagon.

Packing with animals is about rediscovery, too. In our paved environment we've lost that privilege our forefathers knew of interdependence and teamwork with animals. To retrieve it in the backcountry is an ultimate life experience. It's what this book is about.

We'll look at some of the most satisfying adventures this overcrowded world still offers, at supplementing backpacking trips with four-legged muscle, at riding horseback with a minimum of gear, at packing with light, efficient gear. Always we'll focus on treading lightly and leaving little, if any, trace, so that those who follow us may enjoy nature as we have.

1

Paws, Toes, and Hooves: Backpacker's Companions

Some years ago three men, a boy, and a dog wound up the switchbacks toward Sundance Pass in south-central Montana. At 10,000 feet above sea level they paused for a drink of water and a few mouthfuls of gorp. Even at this elevation, it was warm.

The men, two friends and myself, differed greatly in civilian occupation but shared a penchant for anything involving the backcountry. As members of the same Marine Reserve unit, we were able to find excuses for additional trips because we wanted to "recon" likely spots for future drills. That's what we were doing now—checking out the twenty-mile course our company would hike over the very next week. Along the way we enjoyed the area's aesthetic qualities and found time to eat a brook trout or two while we were at it. The boy with us was my son David, age nine, already a seasoned backpacker.

The dog, a three-year-old Alaskan malamute named Smokey, was no idle spectator on this trek over the pass. Like us, he was tired—tired enough to be glad for the rest, for he also carried food and shelter on his back in nylon packs we had sewn from a Frostline kit. Although the kit proved excellent, its catalog description obviously had been written by someone who knew little about the history of canine pack animals. Condescendingly, it said, "With these packs Fido can come along and carry his lunch."

Lunch, indeed. Smokey's packs included a three-day supply of dog food, a poncho for David and another for me, the rain fly for our four-man tent, and two wool shirts we wished to keep handy in case the weather turned cool. Smokey thus fulfilled a role familiar to anyone who has backpacked with a child. While children can carry decent loads, their capac-

3

ity falls short of the added weight requirements they bring to the party. Smokey carried everything he needed plus a portion of the gear one of us would have had to carry in his absence. This is one of the best reasons to look for a backpacker's companion, be it dog, burro, pony, goat, or llama.

Dogs

Those new to pack dogs often greet the idea with bemused interest. It sounds cute but not wholly practical. Yet, as prehistoric people quickly discovered, a strong dog's capacity for work is astounding. Even after Indians on the Great Plains acquired horses, dogs continued to move a high percentage of their belongings on their frequent moves. The eminently practical dogs carried the Indians' packs and drug their travois from camp to camp. The canines could live off the land as readily as horses could, though they needed considerably more protein; for that dietary requirement, the Indians fed their dogs the less desirable cuts of meat from the animals they were hunting.

Eskimos and Indians up north used dogs for similar double duty—pulling sleds during winter and toting packs when the snow slipped from the tundra. Written accounts tell of Indian dogs in recent times packing such incredible loads as an entire fifty-pound sack of flour, split in half to balance the load on each side. But recreationalists don't depend on their four-legged friends for survival; we need not push an animal so hard.

One-third of the dog's weight is a reasonable load for a healthy, mature animal, or one-fourth if the animal is not yet hardened in. This portion of a fifty-pound dog's weight may sound inconsequential to a traditional horse packer; but those of us who have made agonizing choices when loading our backpacks, resorting even to cutting bars of soap in half and sawing the handles off our toothbrushes, know that ten pounds can make the difference between a severely Spartan camp and one of great luxury. Those who have paid their dues on meager trips can't help but feel the desire for foods other than freeze-dried, for decent sleeping pads, for space to carry both a fly-fishing outfit and a spinning reel, for camp stools to sit on and tarp shelters to cook under. Later in this book we'll discuss packing these and other items in such a way that animals can carry them; in this chapter, though, after learning more about canine packing, we'll talk about other suitable pack animals.

Some backpacking outlets sell ready-made dog packs, but it's easy to fashion your own if you're reasonably adept with a sewing machine. Dog packs look much like saddle bags—two equal compartments connected by a support strap that goes over the dog's back. Tough nylon is an excellent material, but untreated canvas is probably kinder to the dog. The pack needs two straps: one that goes underneath the dog far enough forward to rest on his breastbone, not his belly (this corresponds to the cinch on a saddle); the other crosses horizontally around the dog's chest (like a breast collar on a horse). Both straps should be wide and padded and, of course, adjustable.

The straps on Smokey's pack were made of wide nylon webbing with velcro fasteners. For most trips velcro works very well, but it can ice up when the dog gets belly-deep in snow, so I recommend using a buckle in winter.

Packing with dogs is like packing with any animal. All the principles are the same. Balance is crucial. It's far better to add a pebble to the lighter side of the pack than to force your dog to put up with a lopsided load. If the pack is unbalanced, you'll soon know it. Since dogs lack the prominent withers common to a good pack horse, their bouncy trot will quickly let the heavier side slip down while the lighter side rises.

Besides balance, the dog's comfort should be your greatest concern. Pack soft items toward the inside, against the dog's body, and place hard or sharp objects away from the dog, toward the outside of the pack. In Smokey's packs, I had folded our ponchos to fit precisely on the inside walls of the two bags, then I put equal bags of dog food across the bottoms. This made a relatively soft shield within the parts of the pack that touched Smokey's back and ribs. The rest of the packing could have, if I'd wanted it to, consisted of harder or less regular items.

The strap that goes under the dog should be adjusted firmly, but not so tight that it causes discomfort. To reduce the risk of the strap rubbing a sore on the dog, you can cut a padded cinch cover designed for a horse to fit over this strap. A wide soft strap is not only comfortable for the dog but also helps hold the pack securely in place. Adjust the front cross strap to limit how far back the pack can slip when the dog heads uphill. As is true with horses, too much weight too far back can be rough on your dog, so keep the weight forward.

There is no completely free lunch with any pack animal; they all must eat properly to work efficiently. Bringing a dog on the trail won't require as much additional gear as a person might need, but some logistics are still involved.

Food is the primary concern. Travelers in the far North of Canada or Alaska can usually find ample supplies of small game or fish along the way—living off the fat of the land, so to speak. The rest of us must rely on commercial dog food, especially the tremendously efficient, high-protein varieties. Usually these cost more than standard dog foods and may not be available at your local supermarket, but your veterinarian or someone who uses working dogs (such as a field trial aficionado) can direct you to the "superfeeds." The beauty of these rations is that they fulfill your dog's nutrition needs in as little as half the bulk of common dog foods, meaning less to carry. And the dog excretes a correspondingly lesser amount.

On short trips of up to several days, high-efficiency foods should not take up more than half of the dog's carrying capacity. As the dog consumes his food, he can lighten the humans' loads by carrying more from their packs. Longer trips may require the dog's entire carrying capacity for food. You can supplement the dog's diet, even if hunting small game is not your bag; leftovers from your own meals are desserts your dog will welcome, just as he will heads and entrails of fish you keep for the frying pan. Protein is the staff of life for carnivores, and fish parts are loaded with it.

In camp, dog owners have a narrow choice. Your dog must be either absolutely trained to stay with you—and out of your cooking—or tied in camp with a light chain or rope you should have along for the purpose. Use one of these methods for the well-being of other humans in the area and for the safety of your dog.

Most backpackers live on the ground, literally. Lacking the capacity to pack tables and chairs, they sit and cook on the ground. Early in my winter survival training in the military I learned to pack along a thin board of balsa wood, which is generally available from handicraft or hobby stores. Balsa wood is very light and balances easily on a snowbank or across a couple of rocks to form a "table" suitable for a stove and accessories. Many backpackers have developed some similar technique to help them function above the ground level. The last thing they need is to have a neighboring backpacker's dog come romping through their delicately balanced cooking area, knocking stove and food containers askew. Do not, as dog owner, let this happen to another human being.

At least as important is the dog's own well-being. It's tempting to let your hard-working buddy enjoy an unladen romp within a half-mile or so of camp, but are you pre-pared to cope with some of the things he might find? Can you handle a snout riddled with porcupine quills, some penetrating his tongue or, worse yet, his eyes? Can you handle the result of a close encounter with a skunk, a development that will literally sour the re-mainder of your trip? Rest assured, you're not being the slightest bit cruel by restraining your dog in camp, whether by firm command or by chain or rope. If you tie your dog, make sure he's wearing a stout, wide (and there-fore comfortable) collar.

Cleanliness around camp absolutely re-quires that you treat dog droppings exactly like human waste. Most find the waste of ei-ther considerably more distasteful than that of herbivores, horses, or mules or llamas, and burying the droppings is the only consider-ate method of disposal. Incidentally, though I normally use the male pronoun when refer-ring to dogs in a general sense, I'm actually partial to female dogs for several reasons— one being cleanliness. The mere fact that female dogs feel no compulsion to mark their territory by frequent urination makes them cleaner camp companions.

On the trail, the same consideration for others is essential if we're all to enjoy those parts of the planet we can still call backcountry. Amazingly, many basically kind people will let their pet (or child) indulge in behavior toward others that they themselves would find intolerable. Dogs that jump up on people should be reprimanded in no uncer-tain terms, and if such behavior cannot be cured, they should be left at home. And the same goes for dogs that growl or bark at people on the trail or act with hostility to-ward pack animals. Watch dogs are wonderful if they are well trained. Well-trained animals cease aggressive behavior the instant their masters tell them to.

Some dogs want to chase deer, and this also must be firmly nipped in the bud. When it comes to animals capable of biting back, such as bears, much controversy surrounds the advisability of having a dog along. Many bear experts contend that dogs are a liability in grizzly country.

If your dog dashes ahead on the trail, meets a bear, shows his teeth initially, then turns tail and runs right back to you with an enraged bear in hot pursuit, you'll wish you had left the mutt at home. But this may not always be the case. Some grizzly experts are studying the way Russians in particular have used dogs to deter or even chase away threat-ening bears.

Of course, only a tiny percentage of our backcountry is truly grizzly country, so this concern does not affect the majority. I've al-ways felt a dog tied in camp was a good deterrent to intruders of the two-legged or four-legged variety. Certainly black bears, and probably grizzlies, will avoid a camp in-habited by a pesky dog. So might raccoons, porcupines, skunks, and other unwelcome visitors.

Most backpackers who choose dogs as their first work-sharing companions probably already own them and will use the pet they have. Others may wish to raise a pup ex-pressly for the purpose, just as bird hunters buy Labrador retrievers. Choosing a dog for the backcountry is very personal. The deci-sion may be based on considerations ranging from size to strength to loyalty; even the "cute" factor could play a role. My opinions are intended only to get you thinking about what factors are important to you.

It's not true that only a huge breed is suitable. Although a Saint Bernard, at three times the weight, can no doubt carry more than a Border collie, can the larger dog actu-ally carry three times as much? Probably not, for with dogs as well as horses, carrying a load is related as much to athletic ability as it is to size. Thus, the Saint Bernard might be an excellent choice, but only if you want the companionship *and* responsibility of car-ing for the dog during all those months of each year when you're home rather than in the backcountry.

On the flip side, a tiny dog is not viable as a work animal. He may be perfectly able to pack his food, but he probably won't be able to lighten your own pack appreciably or to pick up the slack for your child. Where that lower limit lies is a matter of opinion, but I would not choose a breed smaller than one in the thirty-five pound range for this purpose.

More important than size is the purpose and genetic background of the breed. Though some folks may disagree, I believe you should avoid show breeds in deference to working and hunting breeds; furthermore, I favor dogs raised by breeders who use them according to the purpose the particular bloodline was originally bred for. Retrievers and pointers, for instance, are excellent choices if they come from working stock. Labs, especially, have earned good reputations as family dogs. They're strong, loyal, and easy to train.

The Nordic or sled dog breeds are among the best pack dogs, again, if they come from working stock. One possible drawback to an Alaskan malamute or Siberian husky, though, is the dense undercoat that protects them from severe cold in winter. For backpackers who camp mostly in warm weather, these breeds may not be the best choice. Sled-dog racers actually cease training when the temperature climbs above sixty degrees, even though their summer training rigs may sport wheels instead of runners. Of course, backpackers do not stress their pack dogs in quite the same way. My trusty malamute handled summer backpacking with only the normal amount of panting.

Stock dogs such as the Border collie, though small, are excellent choices for pack dogs because they've stayed close to their working roots. Breeds such as the German shepherd and the Doberman rank well, too. With any of the larger breeds, buy a pup that has the lowest possible genetic probability for

hip dysplasia. Most breeders can tell you more about this.

I've already mentioned some sexual bias on my part in favor of females. Besides having more desireable scent-marking habits than males, they also stay at camp better. But I wouldn't trade in a male for these reasons. I'd just try to improve his training.

Assuming your dog already knows basic obedience, training it to pack is a breeze. Few dogs make it difficult. It's wise to keep the dog on a leash the first time you put on a pack. And though you don't want to burden a beginner with a lot of weight, it's good to have enough of a load to keep the unladen packs from flopping around. A Sears catalog or city phone book in each side is about right. Then, it's merely a matter of greeting any infraction with a stern "no," or whatever action you would take if the dog were about to raise his leg in the direction of your china closet. By infraction, I mean any activity that would endanger his packed cargo, such as biting the pack, trying to rub it off, rolling on it, and so on. As pack animals, dogs simply are not allowed to do such things, and they figure that out rather quickly through your normal system of praise and rewards for desireable behavior.

When the time approaches for a real trip, begin loading your dog with the appropriate weight and take longer jaunts. Since we need conditioning, too, don your own loaded pack while you're working with the dog. There will come a time when your dog not only accepts the pack but virtually ignores it. Like a good pack horse, the pack dog will learn to give trees a wider berth to avoid bumping them with the pack. Unlike the pack horse, the dog can rest just as you can, by sitting down, pack and all.

Well in advance of the trip, you should worm your dog and make sure his vaccinations are current. Allow at least several weeks for the dog to recover from such treatments and to avoid any possible upset feelings on the trail. Also switch to the type of food you'll be using on the trip and make sure the dog's feet are in first-rate shape. Then hit the trail and have some fun.

Bigger Critters

There will likely come a time when a backpacker interested in supplementing his or her efforts with pack animals will look beyond Man's best friend to the big critters,

Burros are incredibly durable, and many have been made available through the adoption programs of the Bureau of Land Management.

the ones that can carry some real heft. Perhaps your family of backpackers includes several small children and the load has increased beyond the carrying capacity of the children. Or perhaps your party of adult backpackers wants to go out far and stay long. Or perhaps someone in your party has sacrificed knee cartilage or ligaments to the god of physical fitness, or time and age have made the packs more difficult to carry and camp comforts harder to do without.

The marriage between backpacking and animal packing is such an obvious and potentially happy one, it's a pity the combination is still relatively uncommon. Fueled by a silly sense of superiority, quarrels have too often broken out between those who carry their own packs and those who bring animals along to do the heavy work. The most rigid fringe of the backpacking coterie sometimes stereotypes horse packers as messy, lazy campers who want luxuries without working for them and who use smelly, manure-leaving animals to serve their indolence. The equally extreme fringe of the horse-packing community sometimes stereotypes backpackers as unkempt hippy-types who fancy themselves as children of nature while using the latest in high-tech gear and who would kick horses off the trail, even though the trail was probably built by teams of humans and horses.

Such divisiveness is destructive! Both groups rely on our precious backcountry to maintain their activities. Both must remember that forces far more powerful than either are waiting to pounce on our last remaining wild lands with uses in mind that are far more disastrous than the messiest horse or the sloppiest backpacker.

Fortunately, cooler heads are common among both groups of wilderness lovers. Some among these can see the logic of continuing to backpack while enjoying the obvious benefits of a pack animal that can carry a hundred pounds without drawing a deep breath.

Donkeys

Picture in your mind a person walking beside an animal heavily laden with packs. What kind of animal do you see? Chances are good you see a long-eared beast, homely, but useful-looking. Depending on its size and place of origin, it might be called donkey, ass, or burro. If the animal is an intact male, he can be bred to a female horse and produce one of the world's most useful animals, a mule. But that's another story.

When we think of donkeys (burro is simply the Spanish term for a small variety of donkey), we often picture a grizzled prospector, veteran of a thousand western movies, leading his faithful companion laden with supplies of all kinds but with gold pans prominent on the outside. Prospectors indeed favored burros as partners. Some of those animals left unattended reverted to a feral state and eventually became so numerous that they have adversely affected the native wildlife in some arid regions. Today there are government programs that allow people to adopt feral donkeys and horses captured on public lands.

The donkey is linked to our culture in other ways, too. Biblical stories involving donkeys abound. If a single quality could sum up the species, toughness would quickly come to mind. Donkeys can subsist on little food and water and can carry immense weight in proportion to their size. And their sure-footedness is legend; where donkeys cannot travel, humans should think twice before going themselves. But donkeys are not known for either their speed or their cooperative disposition.

A gelded (neutered) male or female donkey can be a fine pet and companion; if your local zoning laws permit and you have a suitable place, they can get along well on a relatively small lot in a settled area. The cost for keeping such an animal should be considerably less than for a full-sized horse.

Some make good riding animals, within their limits of size and speed. Their reputation for stubbornness is due at least in part to their intelligence, which permits them to become spoiled by an owner who doesn't call their bluff. Aesop's Fables and other ancient folklore abound with tales of donkeys outwitting their owners, then outwitting themselves and causing more grief. One story tells of a donkey assigned to carry two heavy bags of salt. The animal takes an unscheduled swim while loaded, dissolving most of the salt and subsequently enjoying a nearly weightless burden. But the donkey makes too much of a good thing, taking advantage of his owner by heading immediately for the creek each time he is loaded. The owner retaliates by loading the donkey with bulky, but very light, bags of sponges. The greedy donkey wants an even lighter load, so he heads for the creek and ends up having to carry a tremendous cargo of water-soaked sponges, learning his lesson the hard way.

Donkey breeders may quibble with characterizations of their breed based on folklore, but the tale has some truth. Donkeys are smart enough to bluff if a load seems too heavy; for instance, they may lie down with it. But they have, through the ages, proved their worth many times over as tough and useful animals.

Donkeys or burros broke to pack are more common in some areas of the country than in others. Although they aren't particularly common in the northern Rockies, they abound in the Southwest. Probably the best way to buy a donkey is from a breeder, but you may consider adopting one through your local office of the Bureau of Land Management. A word of warning, though: feral burros captured on public lands, though descended from domestic stock, are indeed wild. Training such an animal, even a very young one, is not a project for people without substantial experience training and handling horses.

The llama is surefooted, adaptable in all kinds of terrain, and easy on the land.
—Jan Wassink

Llamas

A less traditional pack animal, at least in the northern hemisphere, but one now growing rapidly in popularity is the llama. A distant relative of the camel, this South American beast is known for its toughness and surefootedness. Llamas are either famous or infamous in disposition, depending upon who you talk to.

The advantages of llamas as backpackers' companions are many. Their ability to function on relatively small quantities of food and water make them economical to keep and to take along as well as being easy on the natural herbage in the backcountry. Another ecological plus is the llama's foot, which consists of a soft, relatively large pair of "toes" with a pad between the two halves. Unlike horses, llamas need never be shod and their tracks are less likely to erode the trail. Of course, the importance of this advantage depends upon the terrain; it might not matter so much on extremely rocky trails, for instance, but it is a great ecological plus on softer ground that may be damaged under the weight of a heavy animal.

Adult lamas usually weigh between 375 and 500 pounds, and, like dogs, they can carry about one-fourth of their weight when they are in good physical condition. Many llama packers prefer to keep their loads at about eighty pounds. Llamas lack the high withers common on good pack horses, but both use similar saddles. A smaller version of the sawbuck is popular for packing with llamas, as are integral packs that include panniers, pad, and frame together as a single unit. (More on this in the next chapter.)

Given the many advantages of llamas, their fast-growing popularity among backpackers is not surprising. But they do have a couple of disadvantages, too. One is cost. A gelded male, which is what you'll want if packing is your only goal, will run you $750-$2,000. Females are not normally used for packing, but one that is bred might sell for $10,000 or more.

Another disadvantage of packing with llamas is their effect on horses, which you are sure to encounter on backcountry trails. Even though horses, like hikers and packers, are mere visitors in the backcountry, they are very aware of what "belongs" in that environment and what doesn't. Llama fanciers point out that horses get used to their long-necked animals after some exposure to them, but horse folks retort that they can't afford to buy a llama for the sole purpose of desensitizing their horses. Some professional outfitters, however, are doing just that: buying one or two llamas to run with their pack strings.

Horses in a pack train that have never seen a llama before can quickly transform a serene outing into catastrophy, and there's nothing humorous about it if the livestock or the people get injured. As the relative newcomers, llama packers bear the greater responsibility to avoid such disasters. When they encounter horses, the safest course is to move the llamas about fifty yards off the downhill-side of the trail and let the horses pass. Horses do not like to be surprised but tend to cope with the unexpected quite well if they have time to study the situation.

One occasion when horses did not have time to study the situation happened a few years ago when I was helping a friend move cattle down a highway on a hot day. I was riding Mona, an experienced and reliable Tennessee walker who had carried dudes for an outfitter before I owned her. My friend rode his steady gray gelding, also experienced. Unfortunately, neither horse's range of experience included a tall, snow-white creature hurtling toward them like a comet while screaming an unearthly cry. The llama came from across the pasture to our right. I saw no more than an oncoming blur when, suddenly, the rat-a-tat of Mona's hooves caught my attention. Before I realized what was

Pack goats can carry loads over the roughest terrain, browsing along the way.
—Photo courtesy of Rocky Mountain Pack Goats

happening, she executed a perfect running walk—backwards. My friend must have had the same experience because there he was beside me, on Old Grey, in the barrow pit on the opposite side the highway from where we had been riding moments earlier.

No doubt there is plenty of room in the outdoors for both species, as long as the humans involved show each other proper respect and do what they can ahead of time to ensure control over their animals.

Goats

Another capable animal some packers are beginning to take a closer look at is the goat. This animal has served mankind in myriad ways for thousands of years; its milk and meat are still staples in much of Asia. Goats are remarkably intelligent, easy on the backcountry environment, and tough.

According to the folks at the Utah-based Rocky Mountain Pack Goats, an adult wether (neutered male) can pack 50 to 70 pounds with several tantalizing advantages. A trained goat will follow you like a dog without using a halter or lead rope, and it will stay close in camp. Like llamas, goats browse on a variety of vegetation, so they are easier on mountain meadows than horses and mules. At home goats are easy to keep and transport. They are incredibly surefooted, and their initial cost in quite low—currently just $300 for a trained pack goat at the firm mentioned above.

Female goats can also pack, though less than males because of their smaller size. And, if you like goat milk, you can pack a lactating female and have the freshest possible milk for your morning cereal (but I'd chill it first by setting a container of it in the creek). Billy or "buck" goats (intact males) do not make good pack animals. They are smelly and generally obnoxious critters.

Using goats for packing in the backcountry makes sense. Although I cannot claim first-hand experience packing with them, my family used to raise milk goats. We found the critters absolutely delightful half the time and too smart for their own good the other half! "Goatie," the mom, went pretty much anywhere she wanted—up onto the roofs of sheds, over cars, and even on top of our Brown Swiss milk cow when the cow laid down and the goat wanted a nice, warm place to recline. I found the milk good, though with a touch of aftertaste. We picketed Goatie with a dog chain and collar, and this worked well. When walking her on a leash, her tremendous strength seemed all out of proportion to her size.

Ponies

Perhaps the most efficient, intelligent, tough, and inexpensive of all backpacker's companions is the pony. I'm not referring to those miniature horses now in vogue—though as pack animals they might compete well with big dogs; instead, I'm referring to the several established breeds of ponies, particularly the Shetland and its somewhat larger cousin, the Welsh. (Not "Welch," please!)

These breeds are descended from the survivors of some of the world's harshest environments—Iceland, the Shetland Islands, and the moors of northern Scotland. Only the strongest ponies and those most capable of surviving on meager rations survived long enough to reproduce. Then, as if nature had not dished out enough punishment, humans found even tougher challenges for them. From the earliest times the ponies were commonly laden with full-sized packs and adult riders. But when England passed its first child labor laws in the early 1800s, miners could no longer use boys to push the ore carts in mine shafts. Ponies took over the task, living in underground stables and working their entire lives without ever seeing daylight.

If there is a good side to this harsh existence, it is how that punishing background

A friendly mule visits over the fence. Most of what is said about horses in this book applies also to mules—the offspring of a male donkey (jack) and a female horse (mare). Mules are tougher, probably smarter, and perhaps a bit trickier to handle than horses.

improved the breeding stock. These little horses are as "big" in spirit and strength as any full-sized equine. Most of them have such tough hooves that the Welsh Pony Association of America doesn't recommend shoeing except on the most terrible terrain.

Some people think of ponies as stubborn and uncooperative, but those qualities are more a matter of environment than disposition. Ponies too often end up in the hands of children, and it takes only about five minutes for them to figure out they just hit Pony Heaven. They get progressively more spoiled with each victory in the on-going battle of wills. The idea of a pony for a child is sometimes more thrilling than the reality, which often means the pony goes back on the market shortly after it's replaced by a new toy. This may be one of the reasons ponies have always been relatively cheap in the United States. Another reason is that many American horsemen believe children should be started out on full-sized horses, while in England the opposite is true; most people there believe the horse should fit the rider, so well-heeled children receive progressively taller horses every few years while growing up.

As an ultimate backpacker's companion, it is extremely hard to beat a pony weighing 500 to 800 pounds. While small enough to pack without having to lift heavy panniers too high, these ponies are strong enough to carry a pretty hefty load, they are compatible with other equines on the trail, they are affordable, and they are extremely long-lived. (Ponies that live thirty years or more are common.) Another advantage of ponies is their versatility. Besides serving as a pack animal, a pony in this size class can carry an average

adult and effortlessly handle the weight of a child. This advantage opens up recreational possibilities in camp and provides a measure of security on the trail should someone become sick or injured.

None of us likes to contemplate serious illness or injury on a backcountry trip, but we must be prepared for such a situation. It's a wonderful feeling to get in and out of the wilderness using only "shank's mare," but a broken leg or a bad case of flu can splinter your physical self-confidence. A pack animal capable of carrying you or your companion out to safety has immeasurable value. A pony trained to pull a cart could probably be persuaded to pull an Indian-style travois. These simple contraptions pulled by dogs and horses allowed the Plains Indians to move considerably heavier cargos than the animals could have carried on their backs.

Each of these backpacker's companions has advantages and disadvantages, depending upon your backcountry plans, your budget, and your ability to keep the animal during the off-season. And, to this list of smaller animals we should add a well-trained horse or mule capable of carrying a rider as well as a pack. That's what I would recommend for an ambitious group heading out on a long expedition; an animal that can carry 150-200 pounds all day is attractive indeed. If you can travel light, you might want to forego the pack saddle and use "saddle panniers"—cloth bags designed to fit over a conventional (western) riding saddle. For some, this creates the best of both worlds: a low-impact backpacker's camp with the ready transportation—in pleasure as well as an emergency—of a saddle horse.

2

A Packing Primer

Have you ever noticed that some of the more primitive transportation devices are the ones that carry the promise of true adventure? Who can look at the graceful curves of a pair of snowshoes without thinking of a snow-clad, timber-lined trail, flakes heavy in the air? The same can be said of a pair of cross-country skis or a line of picketed huskies. A parking lot full of the world's fanciest snowmobiles, however, carries no such promise, at least not for me. What about a loaded backpack; a strip-planked canoe; a ketch at sea, sails billowing; or a pack train of skillfully loaded horses or mules, with saddle mounts snorting and ready to go? What all of these have in common is a harmony with nature, with the wild environment. All can go on true expeditions, far from resupply. Engines and their accompanying smells and noises are not required; the power, artfully and efficiently applied, is provided by nature.

I suspect early men and women tried packing with animals before they tried riding them. After all, even primitive people accumulated belongings that they needed to carry from camp to camp. And as life for the humans grew more comfortable, their piles of "stuff" must have grown as well—as did the problem of moving it. A horse, donkey, camel, or water buffalo must have looked awfully strong. But how could such a beast carry things securely on its back? There's the rub. One problem is keeping the load from falling off the animal's back; another is securing it in such a way that it won't injure the animal.

Viewed structurally, few things are more different in shape than the bed of a pickup truck and the back of a pack animal. The first, a hard-surfaced square box with sides, invites tossing in items of all shapes and sizes. The second, a mass of living tissue that bobs, weaves, and bounces as the animal moves

17

A full-sized pack horse can set a backpacking party free for the summer and be available to ride in camp. This Tennessee walker mare carries a Decker and two large manties.

A Decker pack saddle on a colt that needs a lesson in standing still while being packed.

A sawbuck pack saddle.

down the trail, poses a problem for securing cargo on its rounded, irregular shape.

Solutions to the problem of keeping belongings packed on an animal's back have evolved since those earliest days when humans and animals forged a partnership. Most involve the use of some sort of saddle that fits the natural shape of the animal's back while allowing a load, whether in the form of a human or cargo, to ride securely. Although packing developed independently in all corners of the globe, the resulting saddles look surprisingly similar: Form follows function.

In today's American West, there are two widely used types of pack saddles: the sawbuck (also called the crossbuck) and the Decker. The Decker evolved in the mining regions of Idaho and quickly gained favor with the developing Forest Service, which refined the use of pack strings to carry heavy loads into the backcountry during the early decades of the twentieth century. The sawbuck's origins go back many centuries. Its tried and true design accounts for its wide use throughout the world, and it is also very popular in the West.

The Decker looks like a square saddle blanket with two metal rings protruding from its top. The blanket part is sometimes called a "half-breed," and it protects the horse's (or mule's) back while holding the two pack boards that help distribute the load evenly

Saddle panniers.

along both sides of the animal's body. Pockets in the blanket allow the packer to stuff horsehair or other padding material inside.

The sawbuck looks much like its namesake: two wooden cross frames shaped like Xs that are connected on the inside (against the animal's back) by padded wooden bars, which are somewhat contoured to prevent gouging the animal. It is important to use the proper size of sawbuck for the animal at hand; you wouldn't use one designed for a burro on a full-sized horse or mule. Although sawbucks are not adjustable, a good woodworker can shape the bars to create a better fit. The modern "humane tree" is very popular, and a special model accommodates the llama's protruding backbone.

Professional packers often favor one type or the other so strongly that they would rather fight than switch. As you might expect when divided passions run strong, there are many advantages to each type. The sawbuck is considerably less expensive and is readily available. Although not as strong as the Decker, the sawbuck is usually easier to repair and is especially well suited to packing with panniers, which is probably the easiest method for amateurs to master. Sawbucks come in many sizes to fit anything from a burro to a Percheron.

The Decker is more expensive and stronger than the sawbuck. Since its metal D-rings can be bent, the saddle is somewhat adjustable to fit a particular animal's width.

Saddle panniers over a McClellan cavalry saddle, a good arrangement. Always use them with both a breast collar (missing here) and breeching.

One of the best ways to learn packing is to attend a clinic such as this one sponsored by the Tennessee Walking Horse Exhibitor's Association of Montana and taught by Bob Miller and Edd Blackler.

Because ropes slide easily through its D-rings, the Decker's design is slightly better suited for cargos packed in manty tarps. The Decker also distributes the weight of the load over a greater area of the animal's back.

There is also a third alternative. For the occasional packer (which includes most of us), there is much to be said for "saddle panniers"—two bags connected by a material with openings that fit around the horn and cantle of a conventional western riding saddle. (The panniers I own also fit a McClellan cavalry saddle quite well.) Saddle panniers are a good choice for people who own an extra riding saddle and don't want to spend a lot on packing equipment. Like any other type of pack saddle, the panniers must be used with both a breast collar and breeching. The breast collar prevents the load from slipping back as the animal climbs a hill, and the breeching (pronounced "britchin'" in much of the West) keeps it from slipping forward when traveling downhill.

For llamas there is an additional alternative to the sawbuck: a soft (usually leather) padded saddle that fits under a pair of soft panniers. These are made by several manufacturers at varying levels of quality and cost.

Putting any of these saddles on the back of a pack animal and properly attaching all the related equipment may seem daunting to the beginner, especially when those more experienced talk of mastering the diamond hitch and of wrecks caused by improper pack-

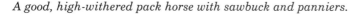

A good, high-withered pack horse with sawbuck and panniers.

ing. But it's really not that difficult, and no aspiring wilderness tripper should ever be bluffed away from learning the rudiments.

Many sports and activities are kept somewhat exclusive by the mystique that surrounds them. Fly fishing is a good example. More than a decade ago I spent many summer evenings fishing in the East Rosebud River below my house in Montana. Although I fished with lures, I admired the sport of fly fishing. But I had never tried it. It seemed complicated. Fly fishermen talked of "matching the hatch" and other mysterious subjects, and my increasingly busy schedule led me to doubt whether I could find the time to master a new method. Then one day, while camping by a shallow stream (suit-

able only for fly fishing) high in the Sierras, an acquaintance gave me fifteen minutes of instruction and convinced me the technique was achievable. Back home, with my new fly rod in hand, I descended into the woods for my fishing time. In an hour I had all the fish I needed. I've been a fly fisherman ever since.

Packing, like fly fishing, is both art and science. To truly master either takes much time, perhaps most of a lifetime. But to enjoy them takes far less. If you can pack your animals safely, securely, and halfway neatly, you know enough to start enjoying this method of backcountry travel.

Where do you begin? If you can afford it, take a trip with a professional outfitter. The true experts in anything are generally those

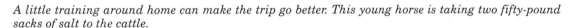

A little training around home can make the trip go better. This young horse is taking two fifty-pound sacks of salt to the cattle.

The belly strap between the bottoms of the panniers should be adjusted just snug enough to keep them from flopping.

who do it for a living. Hiring a professional and expressing your willingness to learn gives you the best kind of hands-on exposure. Some outfitters and dude ranches sponsor packing schools that include trips designed to teach clients the necessary skills. Less expensive are the many packing clinics sponsored by the Forest Service, the Backcountry Horsemen of America, and other organizations. Most clinics use a lecture/participation format, with lessons and demonstrations followed by hands-on practice.

While it's true that packing, like any skill, should not be learned only from the printed page, good books have been the sole learning avenue for many successful packers.

In addition to the one you're reading now, there are three more specialized classics that I recommend. *Horses, Hitches, and Rocky Trails*, by Joe Back, is a delightfully illustrated jewel and small enough to pack along with you. First published in 1959, it predates the ecology movement, so you may have to make some adjustments to its recommendations regarding fires, garbage, and so on to bring them in line with current low-impact practices. Another good book is F. W. Davis's *Horse Packing in Pictures*. Larger in format than Back's book, this one is loaded with clear illustrations, including plans for building pack boxes and other tack. An excellent and more recent work is *Packin' In on Mules and*

Here a light top-pack, secured with basket hitch, rides above the panniers.

Horses by Smoke Elser and Bill Brown. Written in 1980, this book features ecological awareness, and its photos and text are easy to follow. That's enough for preliminaries. Let's start the task of getting belongings safely fastened to an animal's back.

Most of the discussion in this book refers to pack horses, but the principles apply to other animals as well. Llamas, mules, and donkeys (and some ponies and horses, for that matter) usually lack the high withers many of us like in a pack or saddle animal. Prominent withers prevent the saddle from sliding forward and from rocking side to side. Some western stock-horse people ignored the advantages of prominent withers in the early

1950s when they bred "bulldog" horses with backs like giant Polish sausages.

It is important to remember that pack animals carry truly "dead" weight. Even a very heavy rider helps a saddle horse by moving with the animal—leaning forward when climbing, for instance. But cargo can't shift against gravity and move with a pack animal, so it should never have to carry as much in dead weight as a saddle horse might carry in a live load. Most packers consider 150 pounds a good solid load for a full-sized pack animal.

Fit and balance are the essence of packing. An experienced rider can set a saddle on an animal's back, move it a little front to back, rock it side to side, and feel whether the fit is proper. Fit is crucial to the animal's well-being, especially between the front of the pack saddle and the animal's withers. The saddle should just nudge up into the area of the animal's anatomy that widens and deepens toward the shoulders and neck. Then the saddle's bars—the weight-bearing surfaces running along each side where it contacts the animal's back—should distribute the downward pressure of the load evenly along each side of (but not on) the backbone.

All this is far easier to show than to tell, but you'll develop a feel for it with practice. Watch a good horseperson saddle up and you'll see how fitting the saddle becomes second nature.

As previously mentioned, the sawbuck saddle leaves little opportunity for adjustment; however, longer versions, such as the "humane tree," fit a remarkable variety of animal backs relatively well. To protect a horse with a wide build, use a wood rasp to round off the fronts of the bars a bit more. Ample padding can compensate for other deficiencies in fit. The Decker may be adjusted by heating the D-rings with a torch, then bending them to a proper fit, but this must be done with care. I've seen an impressive, handmade pack saddle that combines the best attributes of both the Decker and sawbuck, including a hinged, fully adjustable steel suspension system. The saddle appeared to be excellent, but the price was equally impressive.

Some pack saddles have one cinch; others have two. They should be adjusted tightly, but not torturously, then checked after the horse has warmed up. In addition to the cinches, the saddle is held in place by the breast collar and breeching. The breast collar ranges from a single web strap (economy model) to fleece-lined or otherwise padded leather. Padded nylon is also used, but good-quality leather is the best choice. Natural materials—leather, cotton canvas, and wool—are less likely to cause sores or other problems than synthetic materials. This is not to say nylon has no place in packing: It's cheaper and needs less maintenance than leather, and its ability to stretch can reduce shock. But extra care must be taken to prevent chafing and sores. Imagine wearing a pair of polyester pants on a hot, sweaty day and and you'll remember to be extra careful when using synthetics on your animals.

Neither the breast collar nor the breeching should be adjusted tightly. Their job is to reduce fore and aft slippage of the saddle, but within bounds, for the animal must be able to move freely. Most saddle horses are already accustomed to a breast collar, but they may not be used to the breeching, especially the wide band that fits under the tail. Follow the same rules that apply to the rear cinch of a stock saddle: fasten it *after* the front cinch when saddling, and unfasten it *before* the front cinch when unsaddling. Similarly, safety absolutely requires that you draw up the cinch (or cinches) of a pack saddle first, then put breast collar and breeching in place. When unsaddling reverse the procedure, removing breast collar and breeching first, then the cinches. The reason, of course, is that you never want anything half-attached to an animal because of the consequences in case it bolts suddenly, as it might if spooked.

With pack saddle in place, it's time to discuss our "stuff" again. Some professional packers may sneer at the suggestion that sawbuck saddles and panniers provide the most logical method for the amateur packer, but that's my contention. Panniers are bags, boxes, or baskets that go on either side of the pack animal to hold your gear. They've been around as long as packing has existed. In Part One of Shakespeare's *King Henry IV*, the young Prince Hal and his fat friend Falstaff

1. *To start a manty, Tom has placed a pack box on the tarp diagonally, pulled up the bottom corner as a flap, and is now getting ready to fold up the near side.*

2. *After folding up both sides, Tom brings the top down as a rain flap.*

3. The "noose" goes vertically first. Note the position of the eye splice.

4. Pulling the rope down through a loop gives you a two-to-one mechanical advantage. Bounce it to get it really tight.

5. Laying the rope as shown, then turning it over forward onto the manty creates a half hitch.

30

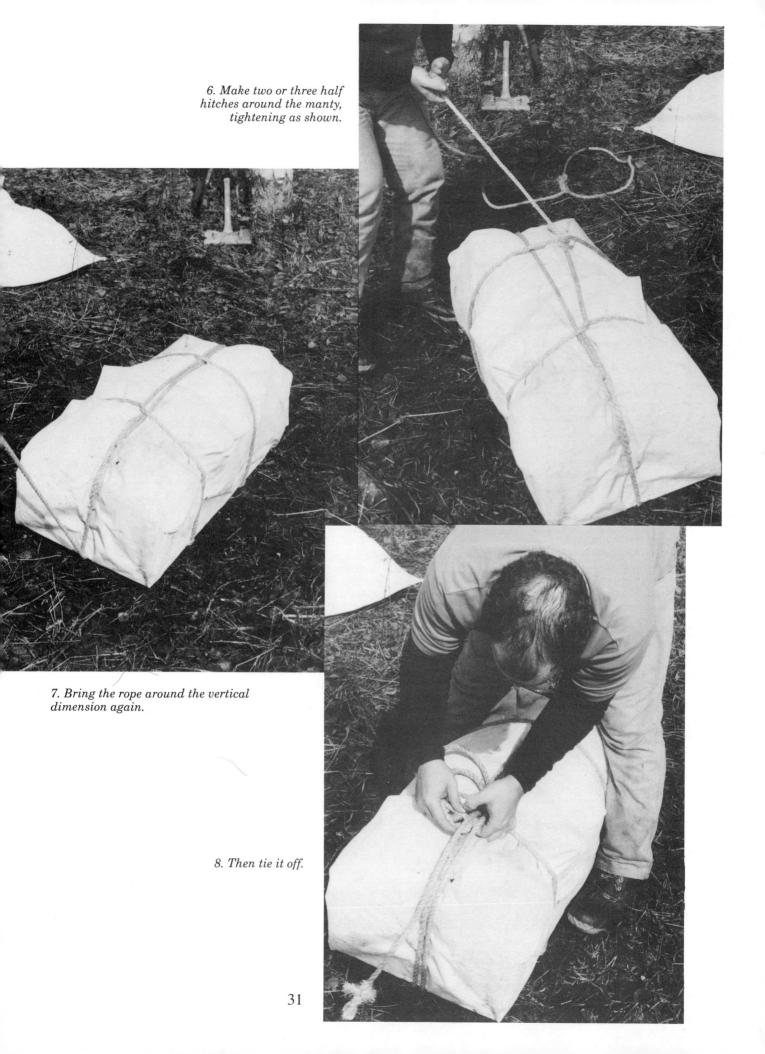

6. Make two or three half hitches around the manty, tightening as shown.

7. Bring the rope around the vertical dimension again.

8. Then tie it off.

1. The Decker as it looks with a basket hitch ready to tie. The loop will go around the front of the manty horizontally, the vertical portion down around the bottom from behind, then up the front to tie into the loop. (This one, the author's, is set up for a lefty: the ropes on the D-rings can be opposite).

2. Tom will place the loop around the middle of the manty, then pull hard on the portion shown dangling, finally bringing it up and . . .

3. and 4.
    . . . tying off with this or another
suitable hitch. Remember, manty ropes
only tie the manty. Sling ropes only
hold it on the horse.

1. With the manties in place, Tom is ready to go. He has wedged a grain sack between them on top.

2. Manties offer more versatility than panniers and are a better solution for long or awkward objects.

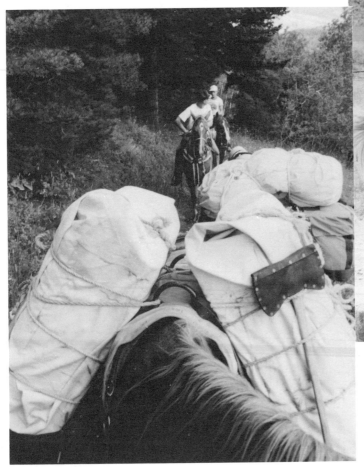

3. A packer's-eye view of the manties and Decker. As long as the D-rings are centered, the load is balanced.

plan a highway robbery of a group that is in the process of packing their *panniers* for an overland trip.

A lively argument exists between those who favor soft panniers and those who like the hard types made of plastic or plywood. Soft panniers—traditionally of canvas, now more often of nylon—expand as the load is stuffed in and are easy on the pack animal if you pack soft items toward the inside. Hard panniers better protect the items inside because they are rigid. Smoke Elser doesn't care for the hard type because of the injury they cause to the pack animal in case of an accident, but you'll find good arguments on both sides.

Panniers of either type have many advantages. Both pack easily and work well when prepared ahead of time so that when you reach the trailhead there's less confusion. Plan the placement of items so you can easily reach what you're after with minimal repacking. Even dyed-in-the-wool manty packers often load a front animal with panniers carrying lunch, fishing gear, coffeepot, and other items they may want along the trail. On any large scale, packing with panniers (or any other method) can produce some organizational problems. But working out a logical system (something I'm better at saying than doing) can make finding things quick and easy.

Packing with panniers is simple. The cloth variety should be loaded with soft items toward the horse, hard items out, and heavy items on the bottom. As with all packing, everything should be snug and secure, not left to rattle. Anything potentially noisy, such as pots and pans, should be muffled by cloth items—you don't want to spook the animals with strange sounds that might not occur until the worst possible time.

The two panniers to go on a specific animal should be as equal in weight as possible, within a pound or so. The panniers should balance so they ride equally high on the animal and are filled evenly front to back. You'll notice if the two sides are out of balance because the heavier pannier will list downward. If this happens, redistribute the loads right away. You must not tolerate an unbalanced load or equipment that doesn't fit well; the penalty will be a sore animal and perhaps a ruined trip.

Once the panniers are loaded, hoist them into place and loop their straps over the two wooden Xs at the top of the sawbuck. A friend on the other side of the animal can help by guiding the strap loops down in place, particularly if the animal is tall and/or the load is heavy. After the second pannier is in place, fasten the bottom strap under the horse's belly. Don't cinch it down hard like pack saddle cinches—just tighten it enough to contact the horse's belly and keep the panniers from flopping out on each side while under way.

If you wish to add a top pack, you'll need some instruction in packing it and fastening it with a diamond or other suitable hitch—unless, that is, you're shameless enough to buy one of the excellent ready-made top packs that neatly strap into place. Actually, an extremely easy way to add a top pack is to use the same basket hitch that attaches manties to a Decker, but to use it hitched high with one hitch on each side of the top pack.

Now, what about the manty method? First, you should understand that just as sawbuck saddles don't automatically require panniers, Deckers don't automatically require manties. A Decker pack saddle can be just as efficiently used with panniers, but it's a tad less handy to unbuckle the attaching loops on the pannier and thread them through the D-rings on the Decker than it is to simply lift them over the top of the crossbucks of the other type of saddle. Conversely, tying a mantied load to a sawbuck is also less handy, for ropes don't smoothly snake around the wooden crossbucks as they do through the metal rings of the Decker. A modification of the Decker, called a "combination" tree, has larger rings that hook outward on each side so you can slip the pannier straps over them, as on the sawbuck. Another approach with the conventional Decker, if you want to use panniers, is to use hooks that attach to the D-rings.

There are many solid reasons so many professional outfitters have settled on the Decker/manty method, the most obvious being that a great variety of cargo, including such awkward items as hay bales, can be packed this way. The manty itself is nothing more than a cotton canvas tarp measuring roughly seven feet by eight feet. Since it's easier to show than to tell, study the sequence of photos on these pages to better understand mantying.

Lay out the tarp and load it with miscellaneous cargo, keeping heavy items near the center while the softer, more fragile items go on top. Some packers place their gear directly on the manty; others prefer containing the assorted cargo in pack boxes of plywood or heavy, waxed cardboard. Packers who use boxes often prefer them without lids, leaving the open end on the outside. The box gives the manty shape and allows the load to swell, if necessary. Once filled, fold the tarp neatly and tie it with a series of half-hitches, then hang it in place on the Decker. No, it's not really that simple, as you can see from the photo sequence, but it's really not that difficult either.

To fold it, first bring up the bottom corner, then fold each side neatly over. Notice that the folds are at the lower side of the bundle each time, where the bundle meets the ground. The top flap comes over last to furnish rain protection. The manty rope—usually three-eighths-inch thick and about thirty-five feet long, with an eye spliced into one end—should be placed under the bundle with its end loop situated where the top of the pack will be. Thread the other end of the manty rope through the loop to encircle the pack end-to-end. Then, with a series of stiff jerks, pull the rope downward; its two-to-one mechanical advantage allows you to snug it really tight. Next, tie two or three half hitches to encircle the pack from side to side. Finally, swing the remaining rope down, around, up the back side (the side that will face the saddle), and over the top, securing it with the hitch shown here.

Please note that the manty rope is not used in any way to hold the pack on the saddle—that is the job of the sling rope. The manty rope's only job is to hold the pack together. Once your manties are built, secure them to the Decker with a basket hitch, a deceptively simple hitch that holds extremely well.

Besides making it possible to pack almost anything, manties have other advantages. A well-tied manty is quite water resistant, more so than many panniers, and dust and pine needles won't migrate into your load. A good packer can manty an assortment of gear about as quickly as he or she can pack a pannier. The manty tarps double as ground cloths or saddle covers once in camp, and the manty ropes have all sorts of uses. Manties on either side of the animal need not be matched quite as closely in weight as panniers must be, because by lashing the heavier of the two higher on the pack saddle (thus closer to the center of gravity), two slightly unequal manties can be made to balance. I doubt there's a set of panniers made that can hold the sheer bulk you can neatly pack into a pair of manties.

With so many advantages in the Decker/manty corner, you might ask why I recommend the sawbuck/pannier method to most beginners. The manty method is not hard to learn, but, as with many skills, you only get good at mantying by doing it frequently. The once-a-year packer may have difficulty keeping the necessary skills well honed. Also, recent improvements in commercially available panniers and top packs have made them very attractive. They fit our hurried lifestyles. One can argue, of course, that we're trying to desert that lifestyle when we go on a pack trip, but the backpacker-turned-horsepacker may still have to fit a trip into a three-day weekend. Recreational packers who enjoy learning new skills and knots as part of the fun should consider the more versatile Decker/manty method.

On heavy trips, there's nothing wrong with mixing the methods. Packing with my own family, I use both methods. When traveling light with one pack horse, I use panniers. If I'm squeezing in more gear, say,

for three people, but taking only one pack horse for minimal impact, I manty up two plywood boxes. If all five in the family go, we bring a second horse. In that case, I pack light and soft items in panniers on a sawbuck and load it on a young horse that needs the experience; the heavy stuff goes in manties on a mature horse.

Well, there you have it. Though you're probably not yet ready to pack up a string, I hope I've dispelled some of the mystery. The resources mentioned in this chapter can take you even further, but the only way to get truly good at packing is to do it, a lot; and therein lies the beauty.

When a horse is expected to carry saddle, rider, and gear, all the weight must be distributed as evenly as possible. Only light and soft items should go behind the saddle over the horse's kidneys.

3

Going It Light on Horseback

Two summers ago I tied Rockytop Tennessee, my gelding, to a small pine on a rocky knoll overlooking one of my favorite views of the Stillwater River valley in south-central Montana. The river sent up the sound of cascading water. On a marshy meadow far below, head-down in waves of green, grazed a moose. A brisk breeze blew into my face from my destination in the high country to the south, and I watched a raven hovering with its beak to the wind.

I turned to look back at my horse. His sorrel coat and tense muscles caught the sun as he stared toward me, then beyond. His ears perked forward. Though heavily laden with a western saddle and bulky saddle packs, he looked athletic and alive, ready to see what lay ahead up this beautiful valley. His pose exuded adventure, a special kind of adventure. This chapter is for horsemen and

horsewomen who are tired of riding in arenas, tired of rubbing elbows with other riders on urban bridle trails.

Thoreau thought we should simplify life and confront only its essential facts in order to understand it. For horse lovers, there is no better way to answer that call than by taking a minimum of gear, an equine companion, and heading into the backcountry. The trip need not be long, physically challenging, or expensive. My jaunt up the Stillwater would take just twenty-four hours. But even such a brief pause in my too-hectic life—one night by a campfire, one morning with the chattering jays we call "camp robbers"—would be enough to charge my batteries for the rest of the summer's ranch work.

Traveling light and alone on horseback into the wilderness is tangy adventure, but it calls for solid preparation and a healthy dose of caution. Although the goal is simple, it involves more than simply packing assorted gear on your favorite horse and taking off. You must choose the gear carefully and pack it right. Comfort and safety for you and your mount is crucial, and your interaction with the outdoors must be ethical, of low impact.

Your horse may be any breed, as long as it's in good condition and healthy. But its soundness is paramount, since there is no chance of falling back on another when just the two of you are out alone. Don't wait to call the farrier the day before you leave. Shoe your mount a couple of weeks in advance to allow enough lead time for an errant nail or soreness caused by improper hoof angle to show up. Also, make sure the horse's worming and vaccinations are up-to-date; such medications should *not* be administered for a few days before the trip.

Obviously, the horse must be one you like. If you were going to travel with another human, you would choose your companion carefully, and the same goes for your horse.

Rockytop Tennessee surveys the valley of the East Rosebud in south-central Montana.

Why spend "quality time" with anyone but a good friend? If you're blessed with several mounts to choose from, there are several traits worth evaluating. Just as a breast collar prevents the load from sliding back when going up hill, high withers help hold back the load on long downgrades. High withers also allow you to keep the cinch a bit looser, which is easier on the horse. While you're in the saddle, you will appreciate a horse with smooth gaits. And since some version of the walk is best when heavily loaded, gaited breeds such as the Tennessee walker, Missouri foxtrotter, and Peruvian paso have a definite edge over other breeds, especially if, like me, you want to cruise right along without scrambling the eggs you've packed. But choosing a breed is a matter of preference, and the horse you already have and like will do just fine if sound and strong.

The horse's disposition is a major concern. A skittish horse will find much to be spooked by in the backcountry. A backpacker carrying a bulky, brightly colored pack may not look human to a horse. (Greeting backpackers quickly with "hello" is more than friendly; the sound of their voices in reply will help ease your horse's uncertainty.) Deer or other wildlife that flush from nearby brush, or any strange sounds, can make some horses decide that all sorts of creatures are out to get them. So a horse with an easy-going, nonspooky disposition is a comfort when traversing a ledge trail on the side of a mountain.

To prepare your horse for the trip, some specialized training might be in order. I had never hobbled Rockytop, for instance, until this trip, so I took him into our freshly plowed garden in May, before we planted it, and let him have his first lesson on soft, safe ground. In that setting, I taught him to picket by the front foot on a line attached to a hobble half on his pastern—a method considered safest by many packers. Other special training might include loading your horse with whatever bulky, brightly colored objects you plan

to bring and taking some short rides as a dress rehearsal for the trip.

Your tack is also a matter of preference. Western saddles have two advantages: an extensive bearing surface to help distribute heavy loads, and saddle strings to which you can tie items. Unfortunately, many western saddles are quite heavy; as an alternative, you might consider an Australian stock saddle or an endurance saddle. Field trial and plantation saddles, though hard to find in my part of the country, are excellent for this type of trip. Instead of saddle strings, these have "D" rings to secure your load. Regardless of which saddle you choose, place the best pad you can afford under it.

Since reins are for riding, not for tying, I travel with a halter in place under the bridle. Often I use a "graze rope," the pioneer term for an extra long lead. Horses function best with numerous little meals instead of only a few big ones, so I offer Toppy frequent breaks in mountain meadows by dismounting and holding the end of his graze rope while he grabs a snack of timothy.

It is helpful to have a knowledge of and appreciation for backpacking to properly prepare for traveling light and alone on horseback. Weight is every bit as critical to the horse carrying you and your gear as it is to a backpacker. A fit person can carry between one-fourth and one-third of his or her body weight comfortably in a good pack. For example, a 180-pound man can carry 45-60 pounds. Put the same man on a horse, add 40 pounds for a western saddle, 10 pounds of grain, and the same 45-60 pounds a backpacker would need in camping gear, and the horse, bless his hard-working heart, is lugging 275 to 290 pounds up the mountain. If you're larger yet, as I am, Dobbin's enjoyment of this whole deal is definitely in jeopardy.

After backpacking, never again can one be cavalier about taking unnecessary items. Even the small luxury of a can of chili can cause your muscles to twitch and the sweat to bead on your brow as you climb the grade. Backpacking has spawned the best-ever lightweight gear. (Although we're trying to escape it, we must admit that high-tech products have made life easier in some respects.)

If you've backpacked, you probably already own a warm, lightweight sleeping bag and a foam pad to put under it. A reliable backpacking stove is absolutely essential in backcountry areas where campfires are no longer allowed. And *none* allow the old-fashioned, rock-blackening "fireplace" rings. I've owned several backpacking stoves and find the Coleman Peak 1 particularly handy on short trips, in part because its generous fuel capacity means I need not pack a separate fuel bottle .

Lightweight shelters have come a long way since the scout-type pup tents of an earlier generation. Two-person tents commonly weigh only five pounds these days, and even lighter one-person styles are also available. Even if you're alone, a two-person tent is useful so you'll have room to store your gear inside. On this Stillwater trip I took just the fly of my family-sized backpacking tent. Since I went late in the season, when the chilly mountain nights made the insects scarce, I didn't need a more complete enclosure. As it turned out, the night was crystal clear and I

It's hard to beat gaited horses such as this walker mare for quick, smooth day rides to good fishing.

Through the gate lies adventure—but one must be prepared for the risk of going solo.

opted to rest under the stars without using even the fly.

The drainage I traveled through had a generous supply of grass for grazing, so I brought only a supplement of rolled grain for my horse. Wilderness policy often prohibits the introduction of unnatural seed, such as whole grain. Don't let a burr from your pasture remain in your horse's tail only to drop out later and introduce an unwanted weed into the wilderness. The Forest Service prefers that pack trains use pellets, which supposedly won't germinate—although I have heard that pellets placed in a bucket of water will sprout; to prevent that possibility, I recommend feeding your horse from a bucket or feed bag that minimizes spillage. If you plan to try a new feed for your horse, intro-

duce it and make it part of his regular diet at least a week before the trip.

I had managed to keep the total weight of everything tied to my saddle, including the grain, at thirty-two pounds, and yet I was traveling in luxury by field-marine standards. But attaching that gear in a way that is safe and comfortable for the horse can be a challenge.

A few years ago manufacturers introduced large saddle packs to replace behind-the-saddle bags and touted them as the best things since the invention of the stirrup. All you had to do, supposedly, was stuff everything into these generous nylon bags and head up the trail. But no one asked the horse. These large saddle packs can seriously damage a horse's kidneys if you load them too heavily; however, they really are wonderful when stuffed only with soft, light gear.

The saddle packs I own have no dividers, which I like. I remove my sleeping bag from its stuff sack and evenly distribute it in the saddle packs, then add a change of clothes, a poncho, and a tent fly. Since the weight is still modest, other odds and ends (such as packages of freeze-dried food) can be put in, too. Just remember to go lightly and always place soft items on the side against the horse, with harder items on the outside. Remember too, that balance is the essence of all horse packing. Both sides must weigh the same.

Heavy items should go in front of the saddle. Many years ago, when Emily and I were first dating, my future father-in-law took advantage of our recreational horseback rides by sending salt with us up to his range cattle. Since Emily always claimed her dad's spirited gelding, I'd end up with Tommy, a stubborn, part-Percheron weighing about 1,300 pounds. We'd load two 50-pound blocks of salt in feed sacks with loops tied on top so they'd go around the saddle horn, resulting in a total load (rider, saddle, and salt) of perhaps 350 pounds. Tommy would head confidently, if stubbornly, up the hill. He carried it all quite well, partly because he was stout and partly because we placed the extra weight up front. Tommy demonstrated what the Army Remount Service discovered around the turn of the century: horses can carry considerable weight without injury if the gear is distributed properly and the horse is allowed to proceed at a slower pace.

Several companies market front packs, and when I feel flush I'll buy some. Meanwhile, I use a long, slim nylon stuff sack (originally a tent case) on one side, and a "fanny pack" on the other. The latter, which I can carry around my waist for hiking, holds my lunch, camera, and some modern odds and ends mountain men might have called their "possibles"—matches, penlight, map and compass, and so forth. The stuff sack contains hard items such as my backpacking stove, which I fit into a two-pound coffee can that also serves as a cooking pot. If I bring grain or pellets for the horse, I divide the feed equally into two gunny sacks and carry them up front also. To the saddle strings I tie a telescoping fishing rod, my ever-ready sierra cup, and a pair of lightweight nylon hobbles. I admit that this outfit has a gypsy look to it and might be snickered at by a professional packer, but it's all secure and comfortable for the horse.

Theoretically, you're now packed and ready to go, or nearly so. It's time to take stock of what you're doing while there is still time to reconsider. Is this outing sensible and safe? Regardless of the type of backcountry you're heading for—woods, desert, or mountains— to be out there, alone on horseback, carries risk. Are you adequately prepared for the situations you might encounter? Only you can decide whether your trip falls within your acceptable limits. Do not exceed them.

Novices often think of being attacked by ferocious animals or snakes as a first concern. In truth, you are far more likely to suffer damage from such innocent-seeming beasts as a porcupine that chews your carelessly hung bridle reins for the salt in them than from a charging moose. Although we should always treat wild animals with caution and respect, most will quickly go the other way when they see a person. In that tiny percentage of our wilderness where grizzly bears roam, I would not travel unarmed and uninformed. But the sad truth is that if there is danger from another creature, the antagonist is far more likely to be a two-legged one. That danger can exist almost anywhere.

Injury by accident is far more likely. Naturally, you cannot foresee an accident; otherwise, you would avoid it. But you can minimize the potential for an accident by

This camp stands in the clearing of a U.S Forest Service line cabin, where a hitching rail makes a handy rack for gear.

exercising caution and good judgment beforehand.

One spring, in perhaps one-tenth of a second, I made a bad decision that could have landed me in a life-threatening situation. While cross-country skiing I tried to round a corner on a steep downhill trail through timber. I had successfully performed the same maneuver a week earlier, on good snow. But this time, on ice, I hit a tree and broke my leg. Fortunately, I was not alone. My college-age son and two other strong companions helped me to safety. If I'd been alone, my situation would have been bleak.

I have reconstructed the accident in my thoughts many times since it happened, and it chills me to think of being alone with such a medical emergency. My only reassurance comes from the realization that I have developed a double standard for acceptable risk during my years of outdoor activity: one level applies when I'm alone, and another applies when I'm with others. Had I been alone, I would not have allowed myself to act so carelessly. I would have scoped out the icy trail, taken off my skis, and walked down.

When alone on horseback in the backcountry, you may have to deny yourself the pleasure of an exhilarating gallop through the meadow. The benefit simply does not outweigh even a tiny risk to you or your horse if it should stumble over a hidden woodchuck hole. When the trail you are following turns into a rocky ledge or cuts across a talus slope, listen to the inner voice telling you to "be careful." Use your best judgment about riding safely or dismounting and leading your horse. Most risk can be minimized in the trite but true expression, "Be careful out there!"

As a precaution, you should always carry and know how to use a first-aid kit. The supplies they contain vary widely, and you shouldn't hesitate to modify yours to suit your particular needs and medical ability. As for your horse, if I could carry only one precautionary item, I'd take a bottle of iodine to block infection until I could get him proper treatment. Other items that may come in handy include gauze (for open sores) and elastic bandages or "vet tape" to hold the gauze in place. Consult your veterinarian for advice on building a light but effective kit for your horse's safety.

Equally important to being careful and prepared is another often heard and too-often ignored dictate: "Inquire locally!" Many outdoor people are great readers who enjoy vicariously the adventures of others nearly as much as their own. But don't rely too heavily on the trail guide or article you've read. You should always check with those who know most about the country you plan to explore. Speak with the local forest service or land management office, the backpacker you meet at the trailhead, and the rancher who runs stock nearby. Any of them might be able to tell you about the bridge recently washed out, the smoldering forest fire, the trail that's not yet been cleared of winter deadfall, and other up-to-date information. Incidentally, here's a tip on public relations: when you talk with an individual on foot, get off your horse. Looking up to a mounted rider can intimi-

date a pedestrian; dismounting places you on equal footing, which is important in a world where friction between backpackers and horse people occasionally breaks out.

Another important step is filing a "flight plan" with those who care about you. Although it's nice to feel free, it's important for others to know your approximate location. Write a specific itinerary and stick to it. If the unforeseen happens and you find yourself in a truly tough situation, you'll know that help will come eventually. Many trailheads also have a register to sign, which is fine, but your best safety net is letting someone close to you know your plan.

Whenever I jump-off on this sort of trip, I feel tense at the trailhead, just as I do when launching my canoe into a stream that is its own world. As I mount up and rein my horse onto the trail, I exhale a great breath of relief to be at the end of my preparations. Then I turn my attention to my horse, the trail, and the outdoors. Now is the time to relax, to slow down. My heavily loaded horse needs a slower pace for safety, but I do, too, for peace of mind. There really is time to stop and look at a mountain flower, to watch brook trout dart in the clear water of a stream, or to see if that pretty rock is an agate.

It's wise to remember that your horse may not enjoy the solitude of woods or mountains as much as you do. By nature, horses prefer open country and the companionship of other horses. If you allowed it, the horse might just head for home. "It's better to count ribs than tracks" remained a popular saying through the nineteenth century. It means that holding onto your horse, even if it hinders his grazing and overall condition to the point where his ribs show, is better than seeing only the tracks of his departure in the morning.

The Forest Service discourages the practice of tying horses to trees, mainly because their pawing can cup out the area around the trunk, damaging the roots. Picketing horses on a long rope anchored by a stake in the ground works fine in some places, but hobbles cause less damage to foliage. Unfortunately, many horses are scarcely slowed by hobbles. A young Tennessee walker gelding I owned actually jumped fences while wearing hobbles and looked incredibly innocent afterwards.

With a pack string, some of the stock can be turned completely loose as long as the lead animals are restrained. The herd effect keeps the others from wandering. But when traveling alone, my rule is to hobble or picket for grazing when I can keep an eye on the situation. At night I tie short.

On my starry night in the Stillwater, I chose to camp in the clearing of a U.S. Forest Service cabin. The presence of the cabin did not dampen my sense of solitude, for the wilderness experience is partly a state of mind. Thoreau's Walden Pond lay within sight and sound of civilization, yet it inspired the philosopher to some profound thoughts on the concept of wilderness. Although many parts of the United States are less well-endowed with public lands and uninhabited areas than south-central Montana, there may be places nearer than you think that will satisfy your desire for a wilderness experience.

I brushed Toppy down and hobbled him to graze in the clearing, then distributed our gear along an existing pole that served as a hitching rail. Though I felt tired from the twelve-mile ride and the hectic morning that preceded it, setting up camp eased my tension. I thought of Hemingway's Nick Adams, who returned from war and felt simple pleasure in setting up his tent and fixing food. I put half of Toppy's grain ration on my poncho and offered it to him. He looked at the nylon cloth with suspicion, then smelled the grain and munched. I sipped coffee from my sierra cup.

In the morning, the chilly valley still in shade as the sun lit up the mountaintops on the west side, I slipped out of my sleeping bag and watched a young cow moose glide through my camp. Soon afterwards I had bacon and eggs and coffee, enjoyed a little fishing, then thoroughly cleaned my camp. I scattered Toppy's droppings, drowned my campfire, scattered the ashes, and replaced the sod I had removed to make the firepit. Finally, refreshed, I set out on the deliciously lazy ride down the mountain and on toward home .

I will go to Deer Creek next June, after school is out and the fields are planted but before haying season makes demands on me. The creek will run clear and cold, with brook trout hiding in the shadows. Purple wildflowers will flank the trail. The colt I take will be nervous at first, scared of the windsongs in the pines, but he'll settle down. And so will I.

Portions of this chapter appeared in "Going It Light and Alone," in Equus, *July 1990.*

4

The Low-Impact Camp

Few among us who love the outdoors have trouble imagining the perfect camp. Some of us are particularly good at this on days when the boss is testy, the weather bad, or the job boring. Thoughts of the most splendid mansion simply can't satisfy us like those of a green landscape with smoke curling gently from the campfire. The image I see virtually always includes a stream or lake in the vicinity, a tent pitched accommodatingly near the fire, a parked backpack or saddle, and a horse or mule picketed nearby. The animal sleeps standing with a hind leg cocked, lost in his well-earned rest.

How we each fill out the scene depends largely upon which things we consider important in a backcountry experience. Some seek solitude, others companionship. You might hear music from a breeze in the pines or from a friend's harmonica. Perhaps the natural night sounds—the hoot of a great horned owl and the trickling of the creek—will be music enough.

Strange, the emotional stirrings invoked by such pictures. In a society where most of our time is spent, as Wordsworth said, "getting and spending," buying and selling, paying taxes, working too hard—how can simple sensual memories such as the smell of a canvas tent, a sweaty horse, or pine woodsmoke evoke such powerful feelings? Maybe the answer lies in some sort of collective memory of our species, memory of simpler (if not necessarily easier) times.

Regardless of the reasons, many of us feel a periodic need to live closer to nature, to rid ourselves of concrete and plastic and telephone and television. Camping has long been the answer. But in our complicated times, even camping has become artificial, plastic. Recreational vehicles, for instance, are comfortable and practical for travel but far removed from a down-to-earth backcountry experience. To better understand our camping options, some of us read and write books—like this one—about travel in the wilderness and backcountry where we hope to escape all civilized concerns.

But can we escape the modern world? In a globe so overpopulated by one species (ours), the answer is "no." We can, however, create or re-create outdoor experiences to satisfy our needs, and that is partly what this book is about. But we cannot for one instant forget that the lands we call "backcountry" and "wilderness" are neither as vast nor as untouched as they once were. And unless we treat what's left exactly as we'd expect guests to treat our living rooms and back yards, we'll soon lose the opportunity to achieve that periodic renewal the backcountry offers.

Americans have a relative abundance of unspoiled lands, and even more lie to the north in Canada. The residents of many countries don't have it so good. In the United States, our system of national parks and forests, other federally owned lands, and areas of designated wilderness offer us many opportunities to visit the backcountry, though there is irony even here. In Montana, and no doubt elsewhere, once an area is officially designated as wilderness, it tends to become less so; the classification and attendant publicity attract more visitors than ever. As a result, some of my favorite backcountry lies on the fringes of official wilderness, on lands managed for "multiple-use" by the U.S. Forest Service or Bureau of Land Management.

A near-perfect camp, with shade, water, and belly-deep grass for the horses.

Wilderness is partly a state of mind. Does this cabin, once a line shack for cowboys wintering out with cattle, destroy the solitude, or enhance it?

Since the sight of an occasional jeep track doesn't bother me, and I feel no hostility whatsoever toward that animal that has mothered mankind for many thousand years, the cow, I know places where I can pack for days, usually without running into another human being.

For me, a typical American Westerner, the presence of too many people tends to chill my backcountry experience. But my perspective is relative. In contrast, I recall the perspective of a Japanese exchange student who came to our small Montana town and was told by her ranch-family hosts that the Christmas season would bring "wall-to-wall" crowds to the shopping mall in Billings. On a busy weekend near the holiday they all went to the mall, which suffered no lack of busi-

ness. After an hour of what seemed like constant pushing and shoving to the Montanans, the exchange student asked, to her hosts' astonishment, where all the people were. To her, the crowds were relatively sparse.

Although most of us prefer unadulterated nature, signs of earlier human habitation need not spoil our backcountry experience, as long as the signs are somewhat attractive and organic. The Forest Service recently took an extreme measure in removing signs of human existence from the wilderness by destroying dozens of log cabins throughout western forests. Many of these buildings were charming, and some might have saved lives in emergency situations. Part of our western tradition has allowed the use of these cabins on the trust principle—if you eat food and burn firewood stored in the cabin, you replenish the supply for the next guy. We can only hope the folks who advocated burning these shelters would not have done the same to Thoreau's cabin at Walden Pond. If *any* sign of human existence can ruin a wilderness experience, where do we draw the line? Is the experience ruined by your backpack leaning against a tree or by your own reflection in a stream? (Ironically, the Forest Service has begun funding restoration projects to preserve some of the remaining wilderness cabins.)

But something we all agree on is the sense of revulsion we feel upon seeing an aluminum can carelessly tossed aside in a place we believed to be pristine. And most of us have walked into a delightful glade at one time or another and found, instead of the sweet scent of flowers, the unsightly appearance and foul smell of human feces, thoughtlessly left unburied. While most wilderness users have improved in these respects, we still use many nonbiodegradable products that require some extra effort to dispose of properly.

The Indians and mountain men of the Old West did not practice minimal-impact camping, no matter how romantically we may pretend that they did. A Crow woman once told an interviewer that the plains Indians often moved their camps because they had either depleted the easily accessible supplies of firewood or the place simply got to smelling too foul. What remained after a move might have looked like a mess, but it was a biodegradable mess. Everything they discarded was organic in origin. The Indians and mountain men did not have plastic bags, aluminum cans, and other long-lived synthetic materials.

Later, when the earliest canned foods started appearing on backcountry scenes, garbage disposal still was not a major issue because the cans were made of low-grade,

easily rusted steel. Even early in the twentieth century, wilderness packers solved their garbage problem simply by digging a pit and burying everything somewhere behind the main tent. Although these more modern leavings took a little longer to decompose than products made strictly from plants and animals, most of them were at least somewhat biodegradable and the garbage-pit system of disposal was widely accepted.

But times have changed. Too much of what we throw away today will not decay for many years. Our heavy use of the remaining backcountry areas cannot be coupled with on-site disposal of trash, so the standard policy these days is "pack it in, pack it out." We can't afford to do less.

Minimum-impact camping, whether with or without pack animals, must address several basic concerns. Humans and domestic animals can disturb the backcountry by leaving trash behind, by improperly disposing of biological waste, and by causing physical damage to the environment. When it comes to trash, the watchword is simply "Don't!" Don't leave anything behind. You may think throwing a candy wrapper into the campfire solves the problem, but sometimes the wrappers are lined with aluminum foil. The metal foil will melt but will not biodegrade for centuries; meanwhile, an unsightly shiny blob of civilization remains in your fire pit.

Pack out all garbage you cannot legally and completely burn, period. Pack for your trip with a minimum of solid wastes in mind. Always take plenty of heavy-duty garbage bags, the kind that will prevent that last sticky bit of soft drink from leaking onto your sleeping bag, and pack them out when you leave. While it is true that these bags also are not biodegradable, that's another problem for another book; for now, they remain the best choice for removing trash from the backcountry. On a recent two-night pack trip with five people, in an area where fires were allowed, our party accumulated just one-third of a medium-sized bag of garbage. That relatively small amount of solid waste resulted largely from well-planned meals and from repackaging as much as possible into our own resealable and reusable containers, discarding the factory packaging at home before we left.

Disposing of biological waste, the kind that comes from the bodies of our animals and ourselves, is a tougher consideration. Here, too, cultural attitudes of our increasingly urban society can play a role, as they did recently when a Florida a traffic cop cited a motorist pulling a horse trailer because the horse inside the trailer dropped some "parade apples" over the back door and onto the roadway. In a rural area, the policeman's action would have seemed quite odd.

Horse manure is not inherently more destructive or less beneficial than droppings from deer, elk, and moose. But city dwellers don't want it on their streets, and in the backcountry we don't want it in our camp or near our water. Thus, most national forests require pack stock to keep at least one hundred feet from rivers and streams; your camp area should be off limits to stock as well. I keep my animals on the fringe of the camp site when loading or unloading their packs. I'd rather lug the packs over to the tent and kitchen area than allow manure to fall on the "carpet." Also, it is a major breach of etiquette to ride your horse into the center of someone's camp to visit. While you're visiting, Ol' Dobbin is likely to leave a deposit.

Since the same camp sites are used over and over by backcountry users, break up the clumps and scatter the manure left by your pack animals. This speeds the biodegrading process and leaves the area ready for the next visitor. Droppings from your pack dog, however, are a different matter. Dog feces is always more disgusting than that produced

by herbivores, and it should not be left lying about. Scoop it up with a shovel and bury it, just as you would human waste.

For many years, large groups in the backcountry were encouraged to dig military-style latrines and to cover the waste gradually as it accumulated. Now, most federal agencies discourage large groups in the backcountry and often limit the number of animals and people per gathering. If you plan to travel with a group, check first with your local land managers for the most up-to-date regulations and recommendations for dealing with human waste.

The rock-ringed campfire is a thing of the past. Now we build a shallow fire pit like this one, laying the sod nearby for reuse. Afterward, it will be hard to detect a fire was ever here.

For one or several individuals, the "cat hole" method of disposal is generally preferred. Dig a small hole only about six inches deep; organic matter decomposes most rapidly in the upper layer of soil. Then cover the waste with the original dirt and the plug of sod you removed to make the hole. When done properly, you can barely detect any disturbance from this method.

Where you dig a cathole is extremely important. In search of privacy, many people tend to head downhill from camp, toward the brush by the creek; in fact, you should do just the opposite. People can contract *Giardia*, the so-called backpacker's disease, by drinking water contaminated with microscopic bacteria. Your part in keeping it and other such maladies out of the water supply is to dispose of human waste high above watercourses. Look for dry, rocky areas at least 200 feet away from any stream. Arguments can be made both for and against burning the toilet paper before burying the waste with dirt, but the safest course is not to burn it because of fire danger; instead, use only white, unscented toilet paper, which biodegrades better than if it is dyed and perfumed, and fill the hole as described in the previous paragraph. Enclose tampons in a resealable plastic bag for packing out with other garbage, or they can be burned later in your campfire.

Physical damage to the environment is yet another kind of impact we must minimize. A ring of rocks surrounding your fire is now almost universally despised by backcountry managers. Once blackened, the rocks stay that way. These fireplaces are sometimes tolerated by the Forest Service in semi-permanent camps that are used heavily and where the pit method, described below, would result in too much disturbance to the ground.

But in order to keep your campfire really "no-trace," the pit method is most often prescribed. To make a pit, carefully remove a circle of sod, digging deep enough (usually about the depth of your shovel blade) to get below the grass roots. Set this sod aside mindful that you will replace it over the pit before you leave. Make your circle fairly small—thirty inches or so in diameter should allow plenty of room for a modest fire. Build your fire in the pit without placing rocks around the perimeter. When you're ready to put the fire out, thoroughly douse it with water and soak all the ashes so they won't reignite, then scatter them in a manner that will not leave the camp messy for those who use it next. Carefully replace the sod and gently compact it with your feet, then add more water to the fire-pit area to help get the grass growing again. After a few days, only a true scout can detect that a fire existed there.

As good as this fire method is, there are alternatives. One, of course, is simply to do without a fire. Another is to shield the earth from your campfire, thereby preventing any penetration of ashes into the soil and avoiding any alteration of the soil's nutrient balance. Tom Alt, of the Custer National Forest, has been using fireproof "blankets" to line his firepits, thereby protecting the soil while keeping all the ashes in a contained and disposable package. Although no such fire blanket has yet been made commercially available, that situation may well change in the near future. Meanwhile, Alt and others are cutting their fire blankets from surplus or worn-out fireproof cloth used by forestry crews to protect themselves while fighting fires or in other emergencies.

Another approach is to keep your fire off the ground completely. Recent low-impact exhibits have demonstrated use of a folding fire platform made of steel. These are currently manufactured by Blue Star Canvas Products of Missoula, Montana. Another creative scheme employs a simple galvanized-steel oil drain pan, available from automotive stores, sawn in half and hinged in the middle

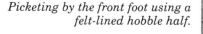

Picketing by the front foot using a felt-lined hobble half.

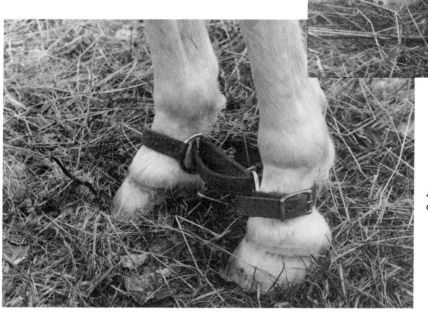

Nylon hobbles are durable and cheap, but may chafe.

to fold for compact storage. This should be used in conjunction with the pit method described earlier. Horse packers might consider keeping the pan intact so it can double as a grain or pellet feeder for stock.

Minimizing the physical damage we cause in the backcountry requires us to abandon many camping practices that were acceptable, even recommended, a generation ago. Remember these points:

1. Don't drive spikes or nails into trees.

2. Don't cut green boughs to soften your bed.

3. Don't cut live trees or branches for any reason.

4. Don't trench around your tent (which

rarely proves effective as a drainage channel anyhow).

5. Don't bury anything except human or animal waste.

6. Always police your area thoroughly when you break camp. Make this a group effort with participation of your entire party. Pick up even the tiniest, balled-up gum wrapper, regardless of whether it came from your group.

7. Finally, don't leave anything behind.

The physical damage cause by pack animals often results from the method of restraining them. Horses tied to trees can be very destructive. In a camp used by many pack strings, where certain trees stand out as the most likely choices for tying animals, the ground around the tree trunks can become cupped out. Trees with shallow roots can die from this condition. Furthermore, lead ropes tied to a tree could eventually rub an unsightly groove into its bark, possibly even girdling and thereby killing the tree. It's tough to completely avoid tying your horse to trees when stopping for brief periods, but the less trees are used as hitching rails, the better they will fare. Small ones suffer most.

Picketing is a common method for restraining stock. Often a hobble half is attached to the horse's front foot while the other half is anchored by a stout rope to a pin in the ground, a rock, or a tree. Some packers attach the hobble half to a hind foot. Least safe is picketing the horse by its halter. You must attach a swivel to the rope to prevent the horse from unraveling its strands. Picketing allows the horse to graze, but the rope can knock down vegetation. If you leave the animal in one spot too long, it will overgraze the area, which will take years to recover. For these reasons, picketing is not allowed in some regions.

Llamas cannot be picketed by their feet. Their lower legs are sensitive and easily injured, so they must be picketed by the halter, and teaching them to tolerate this requires patience, care, and practice before your trip. Use a cotton or soft-spun nylon rope, and, as with all picket ropes, don't forget to include a swivel somewhere between the halter and the anchor point.

With equine pack stock, hobbling results in less damage than picketing, but the method is not without fault. First, hobbles made of nylon can rub an injury to the pastern area. Those made of leather are better, and better yet if lined with felt. One of the main drawbacks to hobbling is that your horse may still wander quite far. Many horses learn to cover ground very effectively when hobbled, and an entire string, if homesick or

frightened, can head right on down the trail without you. To discourage this, you can strategically place a rope or pole across the trail below your camp, but do this only during darkness, when other trail users won't be traveling.

On one of my first pack trips with two young sons, I learned the limitations of hobbling. We camped in a large park that opened in the timber a quarter mile above a bridge and Forest Service cabin. While crossing the bridge, I casually noticed a pole that could fit across the bridge to block our animals from walking down the trail. But I didn't put the pole up at the time because I had also noticed an outhouse near the cabin—true luxury—and decided we'd return to use the facilities before going to bed; we could put the pole across the bridge then. For now, we were anxious to make camp.

We got set up in the beautiful park and hobbled our four horses, then ate Polish sausages for dinner and enjoyed the campfire. We planned to catch the horses and tie a couple of them short before bed. But first we decided to head for the cabin and brush our teeth. Almost as an afterthought, I placed the pole across the bridge.

On our return to camp we walked toward the four hobbled horses. Mona, the old mare, had served earlier in life carrying dudes around the countryside and as a pack horse before her semiretirement to brood status. She looked us over as we approached and suddenly decided the green grass back home was better than spending the night at camp. With incredible expertise, she broke into a hobbled gallop toward the timber at the base of the park. The other three horses, all young and dependent on their resident mother figure, panicked and followed. Though they were less practiced than Mona, even while hobbled they all easily outdistanced us. We ran the 200-meter dash, heartsick, steeplechasing through the timber after the thrashing

1. The end of this high picket line is rigged with an old cinch as a tree-saver and a picket-line loop for leverage. Since both the loop and the cinch ring act as "pulleys," this setup has great mechanical advantage to tighten the line. Tying with a quick-release half hitch as shown here is okay, but the loose end should be passed back through the loop to guard against accidental untying.

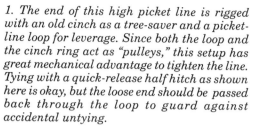

2. Tying the picket-line loop is easy. Make a loop as shown, pass the portion touched by your thumb under and back through where your forefinger is.

3. and 4.
Pull through, and you're ready to tie an animal's lead rope to the loop.

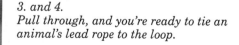

Instead of tying a loop, this fitting can be used as part of a "Dutchman" for tightening the line.

Perhaps the ultimate low-impact restraint for horses is an electric fence enclosure sparked by a tiny charger such as this one.

horses. When we arrived at the bridge, breathless, we found the four horses standing there with foolish looks on their faces, outwitted by the pole I'd put in place minutes earlier. This experience taught me to be leery of giving pack animals too much freedom.

Another problem, both with hobbling and with turning stock loose, is that you can't control where the animals spend most of their time. The law and your environmental conscience may say to keep pack animals a hundred feet from the stream, but when loose or hobbled they'll camp nearer if they wish. (Stock need water, of course, but taking the animals to water twice a day results in less impact than letting them live on the bank.) Hobbled or loose stock will sometimes wander into your kitchen area, too. And I've never slept well with a thousand-pound animal

grazing alongside my backpacking tent, with only a thin layer of cloth separating his hovering heft and my resting body.

There are other options besides tying your horse to a tree or picketing. One is the picket line, a long rope to which pack stock may be tied, usually facing alternating directions on each side of the rope. A simple picket line knot (See Appendix E) works well to secure the lead rope, or you can splice steel harness rings into the main line. One company sells a commercial hardware fitting called a "picket line loop" that attaches to the rope without knots and forms loops to which you tie. You can also use that fitting to tension the line.

The ends of the picket line should be secured to large trees with something that won't scar the bark, such as a "tree-saver" strap designed for the purpose. Cinches from the pack saddles also work well for this, and so does used safety-belt material, sewn with a steel cinch ring on each end; bend the strap around the tree and attach the line through the two rings. Move the picket line periodically to minimize damage to the area.

Most packers used to rig picket lines for horses at approximately chest height and tie their stock to it facing alternate directions on each side. But the horses could not move freely from one side of the rope to the other and they tended to paw the ground a lot.

Modern picket lines are generally tied higher, at about seven feet. This allows the horses to move from side to side under the rope and makes them less likely to paw. The old-style picket lines were supposed to be kept as tight as a fiddle string to prevent the horses from stepping over the line or becoming otherwise entangled in it. The "highline," however, has created disagreement about whether such incredible tension is really required since it is tied up above the heads of the horses. The

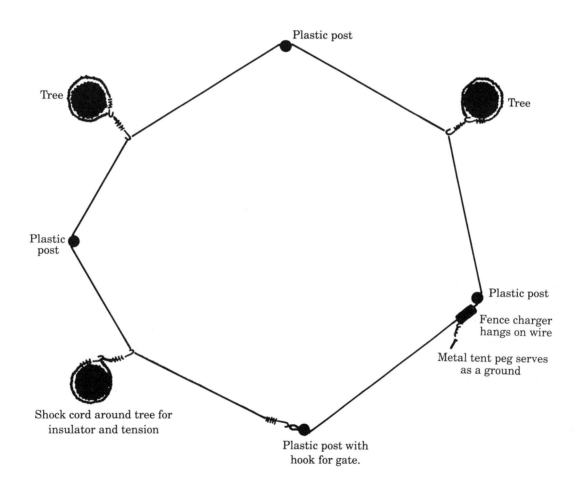

This simple, light-weight electric corral calls for plastic fence tape stretched at the height of a horse's chest, plastic posts, and a battery- or solar-powered charger. Tensioning the tape with shock cord around the trees will not mar the bark and also acts as an insulator. Move the corral daily to avoid overgrazing the area. The whole set-up weighs about ten pounds.

high picket line tied over a rocky or wear-resistant area is now the low-impact system of choice.

Portable corrals have been around as long as cowboys. The traditional version consists of a single rope (several lariats secured end to end) stretched in a tight circle as high as the lower part of a horse's chest. Come morning, the cowboys rope their horses and saddle up. An acquaintance of mine goes on a trip every year with a large party of ranch and rodeo folks who still do it this way; they put twenty-one horses and mules together in a corral made of their twenty-one lead ropes stretched in a circle.

The ultimate modern variation of a portable corral is the portable electric fence. New Zealand and Australia have led the livestock industry in developing a whole new generation of electric fence materials. The chargers are small and light; some operate on flashlight batteries while others use solar power. Instead of traditional round wire, the new fencing material is flat plastic tape about a half-inch wide and available in bright colors such as white and blaze orange. Tiny wires that carry the current are contained inside the tape.

Horses fenced with electric tape at home develop a tremendous respect for it almost instantly. All you need to construct an incredibly light portable corral is a battery fence charger, a roll of tape, and anchor points to secure the perimeter. My charger is about the size of a pound of butter and weighs perhaps two pounds; it holds six D-cell batteries, which last me all summer. The push-in plastic posts weigh a few ounces each and work well. A dozen will make a good-sized corral. Around camp, I keep the tape taught by tensioning it with shock (or bungee) cords. The diagram on the preceding page shows a combination tree-and-post electrified corral large enough to allow the animals to graze. You can easily move the whole setup daily to minimize the impact your animals have on any one spot. Take along an insulated gate hook for easy access to the animals inside.

No system is perfect, and an electric corral has one major fault. Even though you may have trained your pack animals to respect the hot tape, you can't assume their wild, four-footed cousins share that reverence. A wandering deer or moose might encounter your fence during the night and knock it out of commission. There's no substitute for keeping one good, reliable saddle horse tied short in camp; you may need him to find the others come morning.

But the beauty of a large, easily portable enclosure for your livestock is inescapable. The animals aren't dragging ropes or chains across the ground and they aren't pulling on trees. The fence makes them easy on themselves, too: the hobbles aren't chafing and their legs aren't getting tangled in picket ropes. They can make good use of the natural graze and you can move them before they cause any damage. But remember—some wilderness areas prohibit all grazing, thereby outlawing the use of hobbles, picketing, and corralling. That leaves you one option: the highline, period!

The next major concern with pack stock and minimal impact is feed. The critters have to eat, but alpine meadows are fragile and you simply cannot allow your animals to overgraze them. Some districts require you to pack in all stock feed; conversely, I've packed into areas where the meadows grew belly-deep in timothy, green and inviting. This non-native grass was "planted" by seed in the manure of stock that fed on hay. Since conditions across the country vary so widely, it's impossible to generalize about grazing policies on public lands, but you can bet that the land managers in your area have very specific regulations on it and you must obtain the correct information before you take your stock into their management districts.

But the issue of grazing in the backcountry goes deeper than simply considering the availability of feed; if that were the only concern, land managers could require packers to haul in feed for their animals, as fall pack trains on hunting expeditions always have.

Non-native noxious weeds complicate the matter. Two of the worst, leafy spurge and spotted knapweed, are currently threatening the ecosystems of many national forest areas. Leafy spurge has a mellow-yellow appearance that looks benign, even attractive. But its root system is practically invincible, and it gradually displaces grasses and just about everything else. Spotted knapweed has purple thistlelike flowers and is even more insidious than leafy spurge. The jury is still out on whether spotted knapweed actually gives off a toxin that kills everything else around it or whether it simply extracts so many nutrients from the soil that few other plants can grow nearby. In either case, you can easily identify a field of spotted knapweed because of its clear dominance over the immediate plant community. Neither wild nor domestic animals feed on knapweed, and many experts consider its proliferation a threat to wildlife.

Since both weeds are expanding their range, they inevitably find their way into hay fields. When packers inadvertently carry hay bales with noxious weed seed into the wilderness, the consequences can be far-reaching.

Currently the noxious weed problem is being addressed in several ways. Some areas allow only feed pellets to be packed in under

Having your cake and eating it too—the spaciousness of a wall tent without the weight. This is the author's new twelve-by-fourteen-foot model by Montana Canvas Wall Tents in Belgrade, Montana. It is made of the synthetic material "Relite" and weighs just twenty-eight pounds.

the belief that the pellet-making process kills the seeds, thus preventing the spread of weeds; unfortunately, evidence indicates that seeds can survive the pelleting process and may sprout when the pellets are soaked in water. Another approach allows only "weed-free" hay, which is usually certified as such by your county Extension Service in conjunction with guidelines from the Forest Service.

This method seems very promising, although at extra effort and expense since weed-free hay costs several times as much as uncertified hay. But when you consider other recreation expenses, weed-free hay doesn't add up to a major cost. Of course, to be 100 percent effective, your livestock must eat *only* weed-free feed for a couple of days *before* your trip begins to clear their digestive tract of potentially harmful seeds. This additional step should easily fit in with the other pre-trip preparations you must make anyway, and a further advantage to switching feed before you leave is that it allows you to handle any possible problems, such as colic, at home rather than on the trail where the consequences are even more serious.

Along with avoiding unwanted elements in your stock's feed, you must also physically check the animals for other ways they may transport seeds into the backcountry. Burrs, for instance, such as burdock, hound's-tongue, cocklebur, all cling to animal hair; sometimes they escape notice under the tail, only to drop later and start a nasty patch of weeds growing in the backcountry. Thus, your grooming job on dog, horse, or llama should be thorough before jumping off on the trailhead.

Gear

Much of what makes up a good low-impact camp is the gear we choose to bring along. Let's start with the premise that the less you bring, the lower your impact will be (all else being equal). Impact is measured partly by pure tonnage.

On a "heavy" pack trip, for instance, you might bring at least one pack animal for every two people, and sometimes the ratio is one to one. Often we can do better. On one particular trip my family took just one pack animal for four people. Admittedly, the saddle horses on that trip helped with the excess by carrying more than just a rider and saddle bags, and this was more feasible because some of the riders were children. Hikers supplementing their own efforts with the help of a pack animal can probably do even better by using gear and adhering to practices designed for backpacking.

It is a matter of degree, of course. Packing with animals allows us to take items that make for a more comfortable camp. Just where we draw the line is up to each individual. But remember: lighter gear means fewer animals, in most cases, and therefore less impact.

Tents

The first piece of gear we associate with camping is probably the tent. Cloth or animal-hide shelters have long been popular because they transport more easily than permanent shelters made of wood. Wall tents are traditional among horse packers, and historic photographs verify that these have been popular at least since the mid-nineteenth century gold rush. The military still uses them, and some are large enough to serve as mechanical shops for big trucks.

Even today the wall tent is the professional packer's standard. Since outfitters often have paying guests to keep comfortable, they want large tents with plenty of headroom and space to set up sleeping cots. Since wall tents come in so many sizes, one can be used as a cook tent, another for the outfitter and wranglers, and still another for guests. In marginal weather these tents can even be heated with woodstoves. They are, perhaps, the best choice in tents for a semipermanent or base camp.

Backpacking tents are light and portable, but get them large enough for comfortable living on a rainy day. The author's Eureka! four-man Timberline has served well for twenty years.

But wall tents have some disadvantages. First, they're heavy. A ten-by-twelve-foot canvas wall tent typically weighs about fifty pounds, more when you add poles and a floor. Since most pole sets for wall tents are too long to be packed by horses, outfitters often used to cut lodgepole pines at the campsite. This is rarely practical these days because of timber-cutting regulations. Some outfitters stash poles near their camps and hope some other camp user won't burn them for firewood.

Further, wall tents are quite expensive. Currently a ten-by-twelve-foot wall tent costs between $300 and $500, even without adding the many optional goodies. Also, setting up and taking down a wall tent takes time, which is always valuable when you're trying

to relax and have fun. And some wall tents are made of untreated canvas that gains weight when wet and mildews if not well dried prior to storage. The improved canvases and canvas treatments available today diminish these objections somewhat.

Light, strong fabrics have reduced the weight of some models by nearly half. If you pack with a full complement of strong animals and lean toward comfortable camps or camps during cold weather (as nearly all Rocky Mountain hunting camps tend to become), you will probably eventually buy a wall tent.

Every issue of *Bugle*, the publication of the Rocky Mountain Elk Foundation, has many advertisements for firms that make

63

wall tents. The variety is bewildering and the prices very competitive, to a point—after all, each manufacturer must pay roughly the same as its competitors for raw materials and for the considerable hand labor involved in making a good wall tent. Frankly, I would be suspicious of any company that offered new wall tents for a lot less than its competitors.

Most companies offer a base model with numerous options. The base model is normally a tent only, without poles or floor and without a screen for the door and window. Many base models offer a sod cloth, which is a weighted flap of canvas that projects inward (or outward) for six or eight inches all around the tent to help seal the seam between the tent and ground. Some users consider a floor necessary while others curse it. In small, lightweight tents, we take the floor for granted, but in a wall tent it adds considerable weight. The best floors snap in and are removable, which is convenient for shaking them out when they get dirty. Also, you can transport the floor separately from the tent to distribute the total tent weight into two compartments for balance.

Wall tent floors normally have a square cutout that corresponds with another option, the stovepipe flap. You wouldn't want to set an iron stove on fabric, and the mess of ashes and wood splinters is more suited to a patch of ground than to canvas. Myriad woodstoves are available to help keep your tent snug in cold weather. Some stoves fold for packing while others are made to manty. Most are designed so the sections of stovepipe will fit neatly inside, and all provide wonderful, dry heat inside the tent on snowbound October days.

In an attempt to provide the space and luxury of a wall tent without the weight, some manufacturers are experimenting with light, synthetic materials instead of traditional canvas. I recently bought a twelve-by-fourteen-foot wall tent made of a new material called "Relite." To a family trained on backpacking gear it seems monstrous. If made of light-weight canvas, it would weigh around sixty-five pounds, yet this tent weighs only twenty-six pounds—light enough to top pack with basket hitches above the panniers on a sawbuck saddle. The pole set weighs nearly as much as the tent, but it manties well. This tent is like having your cake and eating it too, but I'm not about to get rid of my four-man Eureka! Timberline.

No doubt, a wall tent equipped with a floor, screened doors and windows, a stovepipe flap, and poles, as my new one is, comes about as close to a home away from home you will likely find in the middle of the wilderness. But do you need it?

Marginal shelters at the other extreme are fine for one or two nights. When traveling light and alone I use just the fly from my four-man Timberline tent. The fly alone weighs only a couple of pounds and serves well when set up as a lean-to for rain protection, though it doesn't keep the insects out. This would not be my choice for killing time during a couple of rainy days. But its lightness is a joy when fitting myself, my sleeping bag, and a few assorted essentials onto the back of a single saddle horse.

With tents, as with all other equipment, the conflict is between portability and comfort. For summer trips, even in the high Rockies, a device to heat your tent is probably not necessary. It is far more practical to choose a better sleeping bag if you need more warmth. As a result, most parties traveling light with pack animals on summer trips take one of the many excellent backpacking tents available. The variety is incredible, but beware of cheap, single-layer nylon, discount-store tents. They will let you down!

Nylon is the fabric that has made tough, lightweight tents possible. But nylon fibers do not shrink and swell with variations in humidity the way canvas fibers do. When nylon is treated to make it waterproof, the material can't breathe and your respiration inside the tent soon turns the air moist and uncomfortable. Leave it untreated and it leaks like a sieve. The solution has long been to leave the roof of the tent untreated, then supply a treated fly that covers the top with an air space between it and the tent proper. This system works well. The continuing development of waterproof yet breatheable fabrics, such as Gore-tex, may eventually replace the tent-plus-fly system.

What to look for? Here, I'm glad to shout my biases. First, as with rubber rafts, don't believe the occupancy label. Just as I would never float the Yellowstone River with a party of four in a "four-man" raft, I would never take a lengthy trip expecting a "four-person" backpacking tent to actually accommodate four adults. Two adults with two small children could make it, perhaps, but a rainy day would cramp everyone too much. Generally, two-person tents are just right for one; tents rated for three or four are excellent for two. The tent industry is still caught up in the American habit of rating everything according to what's possible; thus, there are twenty-one-foot sailboats that claim to sleep five—but I would hate to be aboard very long. In a tent you do more than sleep, especially in bad weather, and that's the rub—where are you going to store your moisture-sensitive gear?

Backpacking tents rely on low interior cubic footage to keep the occupants warm. Too much air space above the sleeper allows body heat to escape the floor area where sleeping takes place; the result of this design philosophy is a lack of headroom in most backpacking tents. I like headroom. I remember too many icy winter mornings camping in my young and foolish days, when my bladder called painfully as I hunched over, teeth chattering, to pull on my frozen clothing and stiff boots. How I longed to stand instead!

Manufacturers of backpacking tents should note the increasing popularity of sheepherder or "spike" tents (named after spike camps located away from base camps). These pyramid-shaped tents have minimal interior cubic footage while allowing one central spot where you can stand up to pull on your pants. Since most spike tents are made of canvas, no fly is needed. They strike an attractive compromise between the wall tent and the backpacking tent.

With backpacking tents, I have no strong prejudices regarding shape. I've seen good ones developed from the old pup tent style, including my four-man Eureka! Timberline, now over twenty years old. That tent has canoe-camped on the Missouri River, has been packed in by pack dogs and on a dog sled, and has perched on packed snow. It smells lightly of smoke, and it kindles fond memories. A friend and I once slept in it during a very heavy mountain snow that made a hissing noise on the roof as it landed and slid down the slick nylon. But I have seen equally good tents styled after domes and other innovative shapes. When shopping, look for a tent that sets up with ease, includes shock-corded poles, and resists the wind well.

All nylon tents periodically need their seams resealed—a fairly simple task. Buy the sealant in tubes at a backpacking store, then set up the tent on a warm, dry day and spread the evil-smelling stuff on all the seams, concentrating especially on the floor and lower walls.

Sleeping Bags

Important as tents are, the bag that holds your body should be chosen with even more care. We're a pretty pampered species, and we tend to be out of sorts when we haven't slept well. Balance comfort with portability. Cots, for instance, are wonderful temporary beds if your pack situation allows, but traveling light usually precludes them (though some pretty compact models are now available).

For most light travelers, the sleeping system begins with a pad of some sort laid directly on the tent floor or ground cloth. Conventional air mattresses are not the best choice. Inflating one at 9,000 feet above sea level after a hard day's work will make you light-headed. Lightweight air mattresses tend to be of poor quality and are prone to leaks; those of high quality are often too heavy to be a good choice for packing. A better choice is the compact (but expensive) self-inflating mattress. This style often combines the cushioning effect of air with insulating value of foam.

Insulation is important because you can lose a lot of body heat to the ground, even in summer. Sleeping comfortably requires insulation between your warm body and the cold ground, not just because the ground feels uncomfortably cold, but because heat from your body flows toward the cooler place, leaving your body chilled. One of the most effective materials for preventing the loss of body heat is closed-cell foam, such as ensolite.

A mere half-inch of ensolite has remarkable insulating properties. I saw this graphically illustrated at a winter military camp. Two marines built a simple trench-type winter shelter, a slot in the snow wide enough to accompany the two of them side by side, with a poncho overhead; this is an adequate shelter if properly equipped. One man laid out his regulation sleeping bag on top on an ensolite pad over a poncho. The "floor" was six inches of packed snow. The other marine laid his sleeping bag over just a poncho. In the morning, after they'd risen (one considerably colder than the other), we gathered around for a pointed lesson in sleeping systems. The escaping body heat of the marine without the pad had melted the snow all the way to the ground; his bed by morning had sunk fully six inches lower than his buddy's. The poor insulation cost him an incredible quantity of energy as his body fought to maintain a normal body temperature through the night. No wonder he woke up cold.

A few years ago I could sleep happily on just a half-inch of closed-cell foam, but now I spend most of the night trying to find a hole that fits my hip. Thicker pads of open-cell foam are more comfortable, but they don't insulate as well. I've found a good compromise in an inch-thick pad, the upper three-fourths of which is open-cell foam laminated to a quarter-inch of closed-cell foam on the bottom. The pad is a little bulky, but it packs neatly beside my wife's on top of the sawbuck saddle, secured only with shock cord.

The next element the sleeping system goes on top of your pad or mattress: the best sleeping bag you can afford. Quality bags are worthwhile. A good one is pure luxury. A bad one can ruin a trip.

Thankfully, the truly wretched sleeping bags—the cotton-covered, kapok-filled nightmares that soak up body moisture and dew until they actually feel colder than the night air—are now pretty much a thing of the past. Modern synthetic insulations such as Polarguard and Hollowfill II have revolutionized the industry. These materials are relatively inexpensive and thermally efficient. Better yet, they do not absorb moisture, so they are warm even when wet.

Goose down is still the queen of insulations with two reservations: its expensive and you must keep it dry. I agree with those enthusiasts who say there is no warmth like down warmth, whether used in sleeping bags, vests, or jackets. Down articles also stuff more compactly than synthetics. But a thorough soaking trashes down into useless lumps, and down articles usually require professional cleaning. You can successfully launder most synthetic sleeping bags at home, so long as you avoid the high heat setting on the dryer. If you do choose down, look at the label. Some "down" bags are insulated with a mixture of down and feathers, which isn't necessarily bad but is less effective than pure down.

A light, portable table made of quarter-inch plywood pieces, supported by poles secured to trees by cords (not nails). On this trip the author took two backpacking stoves and a Coleman compact lantern. The ten-by-sixteen-inch plywood pieces have holes that line up and can be tied in two neat bundles on the sawbuck under the panniers.

Regardless of which insulation you choose, your sleeping bag must be built in such a way that its insulation works efficiently. The insulation must be distributed evenly throughout the bag and kept in place by the way the bag is sewn. Don't expect much warmth from a cheap bag with sewn-through seams, where the loft of the bag is little more than two layers of cloth. Down, the shiftiest of insulations, must be held in place by many baffles sewn between the layers. Synthetics sometimes come in mat form, so other systems can be used. Offset seam construction uses batts sewn to the cloth but with the seams offset so that one sewn-through seam is covered by a batt of insulation, not left naked.

Reliable manufacturers of sleeping bags usually publish fairly complete data in their catalogs. These figures consist of loft (thickness when left to fluff), type of construction, percentage of insulation on top versus bottom of the bag (many manufacturers put over half the fill on top, assuming you'll lay the bag over a good pad), and a temperature rating. Read the small print on the temperature rating. A bag rated for minus twenty degrees usually says the rating is for a normal healthy individual based on six hours of sleep. In cold conditions your body loses heat all night. Experienced winter campers never go to bed early, even though darkness may come in late afternoon. They stand around the fire and eat!

Plywood pack boxes help organize gear and make for a neat manty; then, inverted, the same pack boxes make dandy tables.

Go to bed early and you'll wake up at two in the morning, cold.

Take the ratings on your sleeping bag with a grain of salt, but don't buy a true winter bag unless you actually need it. It will be bulkier than a moderate-temperature rated bag and more expensive. But my experience camping high in the Rocky Mountains means I lean on the cold side in selecting a bag. At high altitudes, frost is common, even in midsummer, and a storm can bring snow anytime. A snug sleeping bag is fine comfort.

A down, dead log and a tarp make a shelter for gear, and a poncho protects a saddle from the rain.

On a larger trip, organization of gear becomes more important. Here a dead log keeps the saddles off the ground and can be covered with a tarp at night.

Stoves

Hopeless romantics who eschew the idea of cooking outdoors over anything but an open fire still exist. Such folks fit into several categories: some are not environmentally conscious and/or not aware that fires aren't always legal; others have never been on a week-long trip where the rain never ceased.

I can't imagine going into the backcountry without at least one good stove. The Swedish Svea and Optimus models were among the first of the tiny stoves that I found reliable and hot, and both companies still make excellent ones. Before that I used Sterno and, in the military, heat tabs.

Backpacking stoves have steadily improved in the last twenty years. The old Sveas had no pump and had to be primed in cold weather. They also tipped over easily. Most

The folding canvas bucket, good for grain, water, whatever.

light stoves now have pumps, and their heat output is amazing. The MSR stove uses the fuel bottle as its tank. Coleman, formerly the maker of only heavy "station-wagon" camping equipment, got with the program a few years ago and now makes an excellent small stove, the Peak 1. I now own two of them, and the later model is much improved over the first one I bought.

I prefer the white gas models over small stoves using bottled gas cartridges. The latter require you to pack out the used canisters, and they are not reliable in cold weather. The versatility of liquid fuel stoves has greatly improved nowadays, with some models available that burn plain unleaded gasoline and kerosene (a plus if you ever plan to pack outside the U.S. or Canada).

A valid question when traveling light is, how much stove do we need? That depends on many things, of course, but I've settled on a "system" I'll share with you for whatever it's worth. When traveling alone I take one stove—the better of my two backpacking stoves. If going solo on a winter camping trip, where the quality of my stove and therefore my ability to keep warm liquids flowing into my body was directly related to my survival, I would take two backpacking stoves.

On trips with two or more people, I take two backpacking stoves (one to keep the water hot while the other cooks a one-pot meal), and so that I'll have a back-up. This system has worked well on all of my lighter pack trips with up to four people. On one trip, however, with five people, I mantied the old two-burner Coleman camp range (the smaller of the two models Coleman has made for many years). It fit neatly into a plywood pack box, and its tank holds enough fuel to cook three or four meals. Further, its metal case allowed ample room to haul all sorts of miscellaneous items inside. All things considered, the two-burner stove is only marginally less compact than my two backpacking models, each packed in two-pound coffee cans; and the bigger stove burns hotter, is more stable, and protects its burners better from the wind. Overall, it's a happy case where the more luxurious item is really just about as practical.

Fuel for whichever stove you choose should be carried in the excellent all-metal, screw-top bottles now universally available for the purpose. My scarred and dented bottles have never leaked. The only failure I've had was when I filled a bottle too full in warm weather. When I stopped at noon and pulled a candy bar from my pack, the smell of gas clued me that something was wrong. The expanding fuel had widened the mouth of the bottle, and its screw top easily slid into the opening without turning. Although I ruined this bottle, I learned not to overfill others with fuel.

Other Kitchen Equipment

Assembling a camp kitchen is a process that improves over time as you select and reject articles according to your eating and cooking habits. For primary cookware, we usually take one large Teflon frying pan with a folding handle, and we've managed to keep the plastic cover that came with it, which has protected the non-stick surface quite well. One saucepan is plenty for us. In very light camps, I use the coffee can that holds my backpack stove as a saucepan. A water bag or folding canvas bucket is handy for keeping a supply of water near the cooking area.

A flat, level utility surface up off the ground is a cooking luxury worth the effort. For years I packed six pieces of quarter-inch plywood, each a foot wide and about thirty inches long. I stacked these and drilled large matching holes into them so I could lash them together into two stacks of three, then I tied them, one stack on each side, under the sawbucks of the pack saddle. They took up little room and did not interfere with hanging a pannier on each side. Nor would they have

interfered with a top pack. In camp, these panels of plywood were jewels. I could use them singly or together to form one or more "tables." Sometimes I set them on rocks. Other times I set them across two (down and dead) poles lashed horizontally on either side of two trees not far apart. Either way, the resulting table was sometimes a little shaky but passable.

For years I schemed a roll-up table made of wood slats, but I never found the time to build it. Now an excellent "Rollatable" is available that embodies the spirit of my plan. Wood slats enclosed in vinyl unroll and are supported underneath with an aluminum frame and screw-in aluminum legs. This portable table measures thirty-two inches square and is the best I've seen, and it packs compactly. I'd never take it if traveling light and alone, but for a party large enough to make cooking a complicated endeavor, the thing is a joy.

Another camp item that has worked well for us is the half-sized gasoline lantern marketed by Coleman. I have a larger lantern and never considered taking it along. But this half-sized model is another story. I've packed mine in its plastic case on half a dozen trips and have replaced its mantle exactly once. Although it is an item I might leave behind on a summer trip, when the daylight lingers into the night and my tiny Maglite flashlight provides the little light I need to get into bed, I would be sure to include the lantern on a fall or winter trip when the sun goes down with supper (or before) and there is a lot of living to do after that. On those occasions, this lantern hoisted high and tied to a line from a tree casts a circle of light big enough to let me check the horses.

If backpacking with a dog, allowing less room for luxuries, I might bring a good candle lantern instead of the Coleman; but I emphasize that the candle-type must be a good lantern. On one winter trip I hung an economy model above my friend and me in the tent to ward off some of the chill with its heat. We both awoke with melted wax disks all over our sleeping bags. The cheap model had leaked until its candle was consumed.

My boys like to bring a nylon hammock, which takes little room but is enjoyable to lie in with a book on a lazy afternoon. More important to me is a camp stool—two if there's room. The most satisfactory stools I've found also are the cheapest; they have a simple wooden frame with a piece of canvas for a seat. They ride in the manty boxes folded and almost free, except for their modest weight, because they take up little space; the volume inside their frames is packed full. Stools, of course, you can get along well without.

Old ensolite pads cut into squares feel good, warm, and dry when you're tired of sitting on the ground or a log, and they are practically weightless. On a light trip last spring I got tired of sitting on the log by our fire and fetched the plastic bag of rolled grain we had brought for the horses. It molded to my shape and was extremely comfortable; unfortunately, if I vacated it for long my friend would commandeer it, and in any case the padding lessened with each feeding of the horses.

The truly important thing to remember in all categories of equipment is to balance necessity against convenience. There is nothing immoral about being comfortable in the backcountry. The key is to evolve ways of operating that are both comfortable and portable. The "heavy" camp, with wall tent, wood stove, and all the amenities, still has its place, especially in fall hunting camps where an early blizzard can quickly convert luxuries to necessities, where survival rather than comfort can become the issue. But in milder conditions we should remember Thoreau's attitude toward possessions: they can weigh us down. "Do we ride upon the railroad, or does it ride upon us?" The more animals we take, the more stuff we pack, the greater our impact. There is much to be said for keeping our camp solid but simple. Assemble high-quality, packable items, then make yourself a good list that can evolve and improve with every trip.

5

Kids on the Trail

In my mind are many pictures, mental photo albums, accumulated and indelibly etched from a life spent, whenever possible, outdoors. One very clear image is of a dark, six-year-old boy, a muscular child with the build of a little man. He is wearing cotton shorts, a yellow shirt, and a colorful, brimmed, indescribable hat. On his back is a little orange pack frame. Beside him is a short-haired black dog named Friendly, half weimaraner and half Samoyed, but looking a lot like a Lab. The dog sits happily panting, his blue packs sluffed back and resting on the ground. The two pose for my picture on a rocky knob jutting out from the trail on the side of a broad green valley. Behind them, a half-mile up the valley is a blue backdrop: Sioux Charley Lake.

The boy is my son, David. I introduced him to backpacking early. It was a permanent introduction made possible by his rapidly developing body, larger and stronger than average. David carried loads heavier than I would have allowed for his brothers at a similar age, but I paid very careful attention not to overload him. His pack on that first trip weighed about ten pounds. Friendly picked up the slack, and our camp had all the normal backpacking amenities.

It is natural for parents to want their children to enjoy what they enjoy themselves, to come to love the same outdoors. At what age kids should be introduced to overnight packing, with or without an animal assist, is a tough question. Some very small children are pretty good walkers, and many can ride

The author, Smokey, and David, embarking on one of the trips that made the boy, now grown, an absolute addict of the wilderness experience.

a gentle horse. In a hiking situation, even the smallest child can carry a postage stamp-sized pack, a tiny thing holding perhaps only a windbreaker, just enough to involve the child in the group effort.

Yet I would not recommend taking along a child still in diapers, although the one time I did this the experience turned out just fine. But the situation was a little different then; instead of a trail trip, we were canoe-camping on the Missouri River, on a one-nighter. A couple of friends paddled a second canoe while Emily, six-year-old David, not-yet-two-year-old Jonathan, and I traveled in our high-capacity canoe, along with all the gear we needed. Jonathan occupied a little triangular space in front of his mother, who sat on

the bow seat. Situated there, he rode quite happily, and when he grew tired he leaned back on his mother and napped.

Jonathan, however, was not a typical baby—not typical for us, not typical generally. He rarely cried or fussed, he adjusted well to nearly any situation, and he could nap just about anywhere. Neither of his brothers would have ridden so contentedly at that age. I mention this because the individual natures and personalities of children vary a lot, and these are worthy considerations when deciding what a particular child may or may not do.

While this trip qualified as a backcountry jaunt, it was a completely different sort than a hiking or packing excursion. My beamy canoe carried us and our gear—perhaps 600 pounds in all—and still maintained about eight inches of free-board. We brought everything the baby might possibly need, including a supply of dispos-able diapers that we burned in a raging cottonwood campfire on the island where we camped; we didn't need to live with them until we reached the trailhead. And, although we were traveling along a pretty remote stretch of the Missouri—the portion west of Montana's Fort Peck Reservoir, now part of the wild and scenic river system—we still were not as isolated as I have been on many mountain trips. One boat passed us! And the extra canoe would have allowed us to reach medical help fairly quickly in case of an emer-gency, furnishing the sick or hurt person a considerably smoother trip than would be possible on the back of a pack animal.

The bottom line, in my opinion, is that diaper years are the time to leave the baby with Grandma, if possible, so you can enjoy a less-worried, less-harried trip. Babies are far more prone to sudden life-threatening injury or illness than adults. A case of croup can develop in, literally, an hour.

I won't deny that certain intrepid souls might be capable of traveling comfortably and safely in the backcountry with a baby, but even superparents would still have the dia-per problem. (In an area where fires aren't allowed, would you really want to pack out soiled diapers?) Everyone must face the risk

Steve, while his mom looks on, learning horsemanship as he teaches his pony colt to lead.

For young packers, old horses are the best. Even well into her teens, Mona, the author's first Tennessee Walking Horse, had more than enough zip to get Steve and his saddle packs up the trail.

factor. I considered risk on our canoe trip, and I would probably be more reluctant today. But we were traveling on extremely smooth water, no rapids, yet the current was swift and the water cold. The other canoe could help if one canoe was upset, and we could build a fire on shore to fend off hypothermia. But how well would a baby weather that experience?

If I found myself, through some sort of time warp, having a toddler again and absolutely insisting on bringing it on a backcountry trip, I believe I'd pull a page out of American Indian history and construct a sturdy travois to be pulled by an extraordinarily gentle animal, perhaps a large dog or pony. The animal would have to be led, of course, and its disposition and behavior would have to be impeccable. I might strap the baby into a child's car seat mounted in a box on the travois. But doubts and apprehension abound. In another age, during a mass human migration or a survival situation, perhaps; but for recreation? No. Too many things could go wrong.

A fully mounted horseback trip can accommodate a small child, and some kids develop good walking legs at a very young age. But never set a small child on a horse and expect him or her suddenly to ride with everyone else. A thorough introduction to

The Frisbee is king of camp toys—but get a light-colored one for visibility.

horsemanship is necessary, up to the level the child can absorb. There is more to riding than sitting in the saddle and steering with the reins, and before a child rides on a pack trip, he or she should know the basics: how to turn and stop, how to urge the horse to speed up, and how to distribute some body weight into the stirrups. The child should understand that a horse is not a machine with a throttle and brakes but a living, breathing being, capable of sudden motions when spooked. In short, the child should be well on the way to competency as a rider before riding on a pack trip.

The horse is at least as important. Too often one sees classified ads such as "Kid-broke Arab mare, three years old, spirited but gentle." Beware! There is no such critter. "Kid-broke" and "three years old" are contradictions in terms. A good horse for a small child is thoroughly trained and totally gentle, even doting. An old horse is best.

77

If possible, the child should have a saddle that really fits, not an adult saddle with shortened stirrups. Stirrup covers, or "tapaderas" such as those used on field trial saddles and on western show saddles, are superb for kids because they can prevent one of the most deadly of accidents. Most equestrians sicken at the thought of falling off or being bucked off, then catching a foot in the stirrup and being dragged by a panicky horse that kicks at and bounces the rider off the rocks. The tall heel on a good pair of riding boots can help prevent this, as does a stirrup of the correct size (that is, large enough not to catch and small enough to prevent the whole foot from slipping through). But nothing prevents this disaster as effectively as a stirrup cover, which blocks off the front of the stirrup completely, preventing more than the toe of the foot from protruding through. With stirrup covers, a child could even ride safely in sneakers, though the ankle and calf could still chafe. Most English saddles have quick-release stirrup leathers, and a similar attachment for stirrups on western saddles is now available. (Incidentally, if the worst ever happens and you find yourself being dragged with a foot caught in the stirrup, turning onto your stomach normally releases your foot.)

While on the trail, put the child's horse in the middle of the group. Don't have it follow on the heels of an animal prone to kick, but don't put it all the way in the rear, either. A horse bringing up the rear is likely to lag behind, then break into a gallop to catch up with the others when the distance gets uncomfortable. An adult or experienced youth behind the child can watch for problems—the slicker coming loose, the saddle leaning to one side, and so on. Many horses decide carrying a child means an easy day and will look for ways to take advantage of the situation. Teach the child to keep the horse's head up, keep it on its toes, and walking like it means business.

On foot, most of the limitations of being little fade away as long as the adults are simply willing to slow down a bit and to cover less ground in a day. In years past, many families were led by a workaholic father who had trouble keeping his hard-charging work personality from intruding on the recreation of his family. These days, many families are lead by two workaholic parents who measure the success of a trip by how much they have "gotten done." Putting aside that overachieving professional personality is one of the secrets to traveling with kids. Give an athletic child a few years to develop and he or she will be keeping up with the adults just fine. I know a family that runs marathons, cross-country skis, and bicycles together. I've watched their kids, and I'd hate to have to keep up with any of them.

Strength and endurance, however, are different stories. Both increase with age, up to a point. Marathon runners usually peak in their thirties, and equine endurance races don't allow horses younger than five to participate. I do not advocate that children should go along "for free"; they definitely should carry some weight. But with children, as with young horses, keep their loads light.

There is more to taking kids along in the backcountry than knowing their physical limits and abilities. Where are they psychologically? Just because you've longed for the last fifty weeks to get out of the office and go on this trip, do your kids feel the same? Do they care about hearing the breeze in the pines and the babbling of the creek? Or would they rather be listening to the Top Forty? Parents must not assume their children will lap up every precious facet of the outdoors and glow all over. The whole trip can cramp a teenager's style. And if it means leaving a boyfriend or girlfriend, look out!

So how do you make parting with video games, stereos, and the telephone less traumatic? I believe it's best to go cold turkey. My children know they must shift gears when we

*Jonathan whittles a walking
stick on a shady day in camp.*

head for the backcountry. The outdoors is no place for a Walkman (though I'll admit that if you had to take a sound machine along, this would be the best type because the headphones keep the noise from bothering anyone else). The physical activity of a good trip helps displace any sense of loss the kids may be feeling, and they soon begin to relax and enjoy themselves. Nature, after all, is pretty dang powerful. We really are creatures of it. We fit into it well, if we just allow ourselves the opportunity.

There are, though, some entertaining products from the civilized world that can easily be packed and used in camp that become enjoyable beyond imagination. The Frisbee, for instance, is perhaps the king of camp toys. It is light, packs almost anywhere because of its flat shape, doesn't make noise, and provides some decent exercise. It causes no more than a modest knot on the head if it happens to hit you there; otherwise, its fun, challenging, and harmless. Do choose a brightly colored model so you can find it easily in case it lands somewhere in the brush. Equally enjoyable are the Nerf or sponge bat and ball sets. These too are light and easy to pack, and they're fun for the whole family.

You don't need much athletic ability to take pleasure in them, and they are too sloppy to bring out an overly competitive spirit.

Our electronic world so freely supplies us with music that many of us have relinquished our talents in generating it. A harmonica is one of the most packable instruments, but there are others, too. An inexpensive plastic recorder is very compact, and, though difficult to play well, it is easy to learn the basics of one or two tunes. Practicing in advance of your trip can help build your anticipation.

A backcountry trip just may be the time to ask yourself whether you have ever taught your children the songs your parents taught you; whether you've told them the stories; whether you've passed along the generations-old continuity that is too often lost in today's fast-paced, throw-away society.

It is amazing what a rainy day in the tent can do for a reluctant reader's receptiveness to the written word. Skinny paperback books pack easily. On a trip when everything goes perfectly, when the weather stays good and the fish bite, the books you brought may go unread; but if you get locked into camp, they'll be worth more than ice cream. On longer trips, they'll get read no matter how pleasant the weather. I especially like books of short stories, for they do not lure you into a lengthy commitment. You can catch a story before supper and another one when the opportunity presents itself.

For kids, keep the reading selections on the challenging side of their current level to keep them occupied and happy. Books that are too easy for growing intellects can get boring. For adults who have never read the great American adventure treasures (*The Adventures of Huckleberry Finn, Moby Dick*, and others), a hammock slung between two pines on a pack trip is the ideal place to rectify that deficiency!

Along with these light books and toys, you might throw in a deck of cards, too. Just as the outdoors makes everything taste better, so it adds tang to activities we might normally find mundane.

If you have been raising your kids on well-balanced diets not dominated by pre-packaged junk food, your menu need not change with them along. But most kids yearn for sweets more than adults do, and they may be a bit more dependent on sugar than their parents. Small bags of individually wrapped candies such as lemon drops are useful. Teach the kids to put the wrappers in their pockets until later, when you burn or bag the trash, and the children will learn how easy it is *not* to litter.

I'm always amazed by the number of seemingly conscious people who blissfully flip candy wrappers to the wind while they shove the contents into their mouths. But I am proud of the weekend I led sixty-five marines over Sundance Pass in south-central Montana. We didn't know a tough wilderness ranger followed, with his nose to the ground the entire time. He met us at the destination trailhead and shook his head in amazement. "Not one gum wrapper," he exclaimed. "Not one!"

Some of the "kid food" that has worked well for us over the years include individual puddings and variations on the granola bar theme. Gorp, which we usually mix ourselves in spite of its commercial availability, goes in ziplock bags and, if we are riding, into the horn bags on our saddles. Our mixture contains mixed nuts, M & Ms, and dried fruit. It's easy to reach in and get a handful, and it replenishes your energy without fixing a meal. This is especially handy for kids. The smaller the child, the more often he or she needs to eat; adults can go on fewer, bigger meals.

Drinking plenty of liquids is extremely important when working and playing outdoors. One prime cause of the phenomenon known as ACM (acute mountain sickness) is simply dehydration. The first symptom is a headache. But it is easily avoidable by taking in liquids, and water is the best liquid of all.

Without a refrigerator and its liquid treasures at their fingertips, children, especially, are inclined to drink too little. A portable water filter and/or water purification tablets are essential whenever you go into the backcountry these days. Kids who rely too heavily on soda pop might drink water only when they can find nothing else. Traveling light precludes bringing a supply of pop, but an acceptable (to most) substitute is Tang orange drink, which we usually bring along on our trips. Milk, of course, is one of the staple liquids for kids; we handle that problem by packing the powdered variety. It tastes better if you mix it when you first arrive in camp, then leave it in a container sitting in cold water for a while. Only when it's first mixed does it taste truly lousy.

If you have several children and they have arrived at that age when parents become bothersome, try camping with two smaller tents rather than a single large one. This setup is not as good for rainy days, but older kids with their own rooms usually prefer the privacy. A large family could take three light tents—one for the girls, one for the boys, and one for the parents—and still pack less weight than one large wall tent. Privacy is good for the adults, too.

The subject children like least to hear about, unfortunately, is also the greatest parental concern on any backcountry trip. I am referring, of course, to safety. Most adults

Interaction, lots of it, makes for rapport and safety with animals. Here Justin Carpenter cradles a bottle colt.

have brushed up against the great unknown once or twice in their years of life and survived. They know accidents *can happen*. Children, we hope, have not yet had to face their own mortality; they think it happens only to other people. This difference in outlook is one of the things that makes parenting so tough.

If you can, impress on your children that the acceptable level of safety at home may not be good enough in the backcountry. They can't dial 911 from the wilderness. Carelessness too close to the fire or cookstove means you have to live with the pain. A broken arm or leg will ruin the trip for everyone and result in a painful journey to the trailhead.

Safety is a difficult issue. We want our children to feel free, to enjoy, to participate in the wonders around them. But nothing in life is totally safe. Adults accept that all the safety rules must be tightened when help is far away, but a kid's job is to have fun and try new things.

Preparation for your trip should include a detailed, complete first-aid kit and the knowledge to use its contents. The kit should include items that enable you to handle a vast array of situations: from bee stings to bone-deep gashes, from headaches and nausea to infections. In addition, you must have an emergency plan. Take time to consider contingency plans. What would you do in a true emergency, besides remaining calm and clear-headed?

File an itinerary with a trustworthy friend and sign the register at the trailhead. If someone in your party gets seriously hurt or ill, in most cases you should stay with the person until help arrives; leave the medical evacuation to those who are trained for it. In Montana, for instance, all major hospitals operate helicopter rescue services that can get clearance to fly into wilderness areas, and most counties contain volunteer search and rescue clubs that assist the county sheriff. But to help you, they must know how to find you. They must be notified.

On a mounted trip, consider which horse and rider you would send to the trailhead to get help. I would choose the gentlest horse and the steadiest rider over the fastest pair. In a hiking situation I would send someone clear-headed and dependable.

In Chapter Three I told the story of breaking my leg while cross-country skiing. Luckily, I was only three miles from the trailhead and had three strong men to rely on for help. We were tempted to try to "get out on our own," to prove our toughness by refusing to ask for outside help. My companions, after all, were strong enough to carry

An excellent child's saddle with the most important safety feature: stirrup covers to prevent a foot sliding through and getting caught.

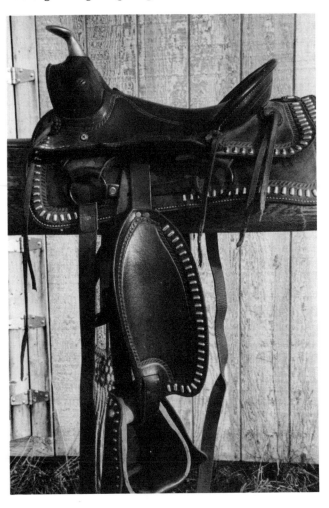

my 200-plus pounds. My son David, who I mentioned at the beginning of this chapter, now grown up, carried me piggyback several hundred yards. But, though my threshold of pain is relatively high, the movement of my injured leg was more than I could stand, and we quickly returned to our senses. I got cold waiting there with one friend for help to arrive. But the smooth ride out on a sled behind a snowmobile, with my leg in a temporary splint and my whole body in a search and rescue sleeping bag, made us all glad we had asked for help.

Avoid becoming so consumed with "what-ifs" that you can't enjoy your trip for all the worry, or, worse yet, that you don't go on the trip at all. There are far more dangerous places to take your children than into the backcountry on a well-planned trip.

Earlier I quoted Thoreau's reason for going to the woods—to live, as he said, deliberately, to front only the essential facts of life. Thoreau had no children. But had he been a father, I can only think he would have immersed his children in the same idea. He would take them to the woods and let nature do the rest. He would show them the wonder of it. Participate, rather than watch, if possible.

A backcountry trip can help you to show your children, maybe even let them taste, such wonderful elements in the cycle of life as the food chain. Never graze on nature's fruit without knowledge, but if you know or can learn about which berries and mushrooms are safe to eat, by all means, do so. Show your kids what nature really is; go beyond the Disney, cutesy, sanitized version that pretends there is no death. When your children eat those berries, bursting with vitamins, and enjoy the perfect protein in the trout they have caught, when they understand that some species die so that others may live, they are wiser for it. They will then know what some adults do not, what some deny when they shop for supermarket food in plastic packages; they'll know that even vegetarians can eat only because perfect forms of life, such as a grain of wheat, die, and that there is nothing wrong with this process—it's just another of nature's miracles.

It is learning and appreciating this type of knowledge that Thoreau meant when he spoke of the essential facts of life. You can teach your children these things in a backcountry environment, close up, for real, in a way you never can at home. Only in this way can we hope to produce a human being who has an ultimate respect for nature and the backcountry, a respect that is its only protection. Take your children along, and teach them well.

6

Where to Go and How to Get There

Last summer our family drove 5,500 miles. Our trip took us from our home in Montana to Wyoming, South Dakota, and Minnesota, then through Iowa, Missouri, Illinois, Kentucky, Tennessee, Alabama, and Mississippi. After a stay in Louisiana we went into Texas, then continued to Oklahoma, Kansas, Colorado, and Wyoming before returning home. When we left, the Rocky Mountains were behind us, and we crossed sagebrush flats where the sun flashed off the white rump patches of pronghorn antelope. Across the northern Midwest we drove past lakes, cornfields, and stately farmhouses on multiacre lawns. Then came Mark Twain's Mississippi steamboat country, followed by the oak forests of southern Illinois and Tennessee walking horse country, bounded on the east by the fringes of the Great Smoky Moun-

tains. Farther south there were pine forests, then Louisiana bayou country, where families in fishing boats catch their supper around the pilings of the elevated interstate highway. And that was only the first half of the trip!

Although we went through some populous areas, I could not help but marvel at the variety and quantity of land the United States has to offer. I used to wonder what my Norwegian ancestors, sea people, could see in far-inland states like Minnesota and Iowa to make them leave their homes for the other side of the world, but now I know: land. Land not owned by an absentee landlord or a rich man who would hunt you down if you took a hare or deer to feed your family. Our nation is very much a reflection of our ancestors' desire for land, not only private parcels for themselves, but public lands reserved for all

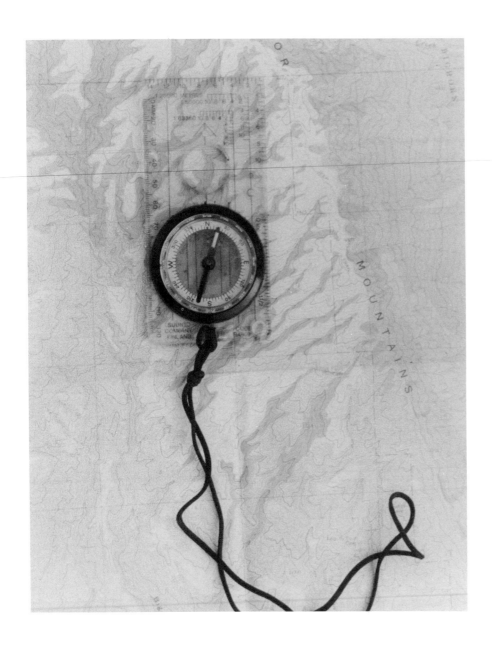

A compass and a contour map, breeders of anticipation.

and accessible to all. The result is an American treasure.

In the search for places to launch packing adventures it is logical to begin with federal lands, and our nation contains an incredible variety. Western states contain the bulk of federal land, but surprises exist. Texas, for instance, contains nearly none, while Nevada has far more federal than privately owned land.

Two federal agencies control most federal land. (See Appendix A for addresses and phone numbers.) The U.S Forest Service, a division of the Department of Agriculture, administers some of our most beautiful land. The Bureau of Land Management (BLM), part of the Department of the Interior, controls vast holdings of wide-open land, much of it interspersed with private holdings in a checkerboard pattern. Opinions vary violently as to how these land treasures should be managed, and both agencies are frequently involved in controversial issues. But both agencies provide valuable resources to the public, supplying maps and brochures of areas under their jurisdictions. The agencies'

The country behind and to the left of the people is "multiple use" Forest Service land, which allows grazing. On this midsummer trip there were few cows, luxurious grass, and no other people whatsoever. Ironically, the trails in a nearby designated wilderness area were crowded. Don't overlook BLM and non-wilderness Forest Service areas when planning your trip.

national offices have listings of holdings in various areas, and regional offices supply more specific and up-to-date information about particular areas. You'll want all the available information pertaining to the use of pack animals on public lands, as well as camping and fire regulations.

Forest Service land falls under numerous categories, each with distinctly different regulations. The most publicized of these are lands officially designated as wilderness. For some people, these tracts of land are the most desirable destinations because of the thorough protection wilderness areas receive from the equipment and impacts we normally associate with civilization. No motorized vehicles are permitted within wilderness boundaries, and some areas ban non-motorized vehicles such as mountain bikes. Fishing and hunting are allowed as tools of wildlife management, but such conveniences as chain saws are illegal. Airplanes cannot land in wilderness areas except in emergencies. Wilderness areas also have the tightest regulations regarding low-impact camping, but those principles are worth practicing everywhere.

It is easy to see why designated wilderness areas are a mecca for many backcountry travelers, but there is a down side to their popularity. Each new tract of land designated as wilderness is thoroughly reported in the outdoor press. Sometimes that publicity opens the floodgates, and some wilderness areas are more heavily used, and in some respects less wildernesslike, than neighboring forest areas.

Don't overlook the vast areas of Forest Service and BLM lands that are classified for multiple uses. These areas allow, under considerable regulation, such activities as mining, logging, and grazing. Some people with purist attitudes might overlook a forest tract as big as the state of Massachusetts because it contains a mining claim, a small herd of cattle, or a logging operation. But to do so is foolish, since such tracts often include spectacular, pristine areas.

I am lucky enough to live about twenty-five miles from four different trailheads leading up drainages into the Absaroka-Beartooth Wilderness Area in south-central Montana. All the trails are spectacular, and I use them frequently. I can count on breathtaking scenery and wonderful fishing. I can also count on seeing people on the trail; however, on multiple-use national forest land a little farther west—a forested, rolling, pastoral area with clear creeks and a tiny, deserted sheepherder's cabin—I have yet to run into another human being on my dozen or so rides and hikes into the area. I have, however, seen the track of a trail bike used by a rancher to bring salt to his cattle. As in many areas where grazing is allowed, the ranchers can lease the grassland only every other year; if cattle bother you, it is easy to check with the Forest Service regional office to see which areas are grazed at which times.

East of my home lie the Pryor Mountains, managed by the Forest Service, the BLM, and the Crow people. None of the land is designated wilderness, but in many ways it is wilder than many places so designated. Among the Pryor range's treasures are a herd of wild horses, Indian cave paintings, ice caves, and hidden cabins once inhabited by horse thieves and outlaws.

Wildlife, too, is bountiful on lands managed for multiple-use, often more bountiful than in wilderness areas. This surprises those who believe wild animals fare better by being farther from humans. But food is always their major concern, and dense old-growth forest does not sustain many species of wildlife. Conversely, cultivated lands that grow food are frequently overrun by deer and antelope. True, you're more likely to spot moose in wilderness or other remote areas, but those areas generally are not quite as good for observing other wildlife as some of the semi-forested country common among BLM holdings.

Another category of Forest Service land is that not yet designated as either wilderness or multiple-use; these vast holdings of roadless areas are common throughout most of the West and are still being studied for future classification. These tracts of land are political footballs for lawmakers and a host of special interest groups, all with opinions about the lands' future. The only good thing about this morass is that some of these roadless areas are being relatively well protected and offer wonderful opportunities for packers.

Still another category of federally managed land is the national park system. Most of the larger national parks allow visitors to pack with animals, but you should expect somewhat tighter restrictions than on other federal lands, since these lands are not managed for multiple-use. Hunting and the use of firearms normally are not allowed, and strict regulations govern fishing and fires. Rules vary widely from park to park, so you must contact the park rangers for more information.

State governments also own land that is open to packers. Many states reserve one section (one square mile) per township to generate income for the local school district.

These sections are usually leased to a farmer or rancher with the state retaining all hunting and other rights for the public. It may take a color-coded land-ownership map (such as those offered by the BLM) to figure out who owns what, but a little research can uncover some jewels.

Public lands in all of the above categories are more common in the western half of the United States, and federal land in the East tends to be more heavily used. But that doesn't mean your only alternatives are in the West. Don't overlook private lands. Timber companies, for instance, often have vast holdings in many parts of the country, particularly in the South. Some private corporations allow public recreation on their land. Federal subsidies in the nineteenth century granted millions of acres to the railroads as an incentive to extend their tracks into new territories. Some of these companies still own those parcels and make them available for public use.

So, you are tooling down the freeway, and you notice the land on your right is beautiful timbered country, seemingly without farms or residences. How do you find out who owns it? Fortunately, it is easy: Go to the courthouse at the county seat and ask! Counties maintain land ownership maps for tax purposes, and the information is public. If you discover the huge timbered tract you've noticed is owned by a timber company, locate the company's address—probably also available at the courthouse—and contact it. Beyond gaining access, you may find yourself alone in a chunk of nature nobody else is visiting. Of course, it helps if you know what that chunk contains, for you can only see a small part of it from the highway. That's where another government agency comes in: the U.S. Geological Survey (USGS). It surveys *all* of this grand country and creates detailed topographical maps, which you can buy. Contact the nearest regional office (see

Appendix A) for a master map that shows your whole state broken down into blocks representing the larger-scale maps available. Then buy what you need. It helps if along the way you become a map and compass freak, as I have. The more skill you gain with topographical maps, the more you'll be able to visualize the terrain and decide whether it justifies further exploration.

Some Indian reservations welcome visitors with a backcountry orientation. Since Indian tribes also have jurisdiction over the fish and wildlife on their reservations, many of them encourage outdoor activities, especially fishing and hunting, for the potential income. This is an emerging opportunity, however, and not all tribes have established a permit system yet. But since many reservations contain beautiful and remote, virtually uninhabited, land, they represent good possibilities for future recreation.

One extremely helpful organization with tips on where to go is Backcountry Horsemen of America. This nationwide organization has grown with two aims in mind: to defend the political rights of backcountry horsepeople, preventing the closure of trails to horses and other restrictions on animals; and to act as a service organization that builds and improves trails and trailheads (usually working with the Forest Service) and educates the public in low-impact packing and camping techniques. Their free pamphlets (such as the excellent "Mountain Manners") are very useful to anyone planning to pack in.

No matter how you get your information on where to go, don't forget to inquire locally! Is the printed information going to be current enough to keep you out of trouble, to report on the rebuilt trail or the washed-out bridge or the new regulation that prohibits fishing? If you are headed for Forest Service land, contact the regional office and get the latest status report. In my area, trails are "logged" during June and sometimes July.

That is, the winter's accumulation of downed trees is removed from the trail. If you are backpacking with a dog, llama, burro, or pony, such obstacles might not be serious, but if you are planning a full-fledged pack trip, a trail not yet logged means many delays and a great deal of hard work chopping yourself a path.

Get in the habit of talking with people who are on the way out of the drainage you are headed into. Talk to the stockman who runs cattle in the area, the fisherman, the pilot who has flown over, and anyone likely to have current information.

Getting There

Few Americans are lucky enough to be able to launch a wilderness trip from their backyards. Most of us must travel to a trailhead or similar jumping-off point, and that means taking vehicles or public transportation. The lightest kind of animal packer, the backpacker who brings along a pack dog, certainly has the easiest time getting to the trail. If the dog is already used to vehicle travel, there is little to do besides opening the car door and telling the animal to jump

The author's four-horse stock combination trailer, a typical western outfit.

90

in. In practice, however, I notice that many people who travel often with large dogs use station wagons or utility vehicles with portable kennels in the rear.

As soon as you move up the line, even to the smaller non-canine pack animals such as ponies and llamas, getting the animal to the trailhead becomes a major undertaking. Let's take a quick look at the most popular approaches.

Although many light horse trailers, especially European models, can be pulled behind passenger cars, a pickup truck has many advantages. Full-sized half-ton or three-quarter-ton pickups are relatively rugged and powerful; pulling trailers is one of the many things they do well. Most passenger vehicles manufactured in recent decades, however, have been tailored for fuel efficiency and are rarely built with power to spare, as the monsters of the 1950s and 1960s were.

By adding a stock rack to the bed of a full-sized pickup, you could haul one or two pack animals in the back without towing a trailer. A half-ton pickup with stock rack can carry a couple of llamas or ponies; a heavy-

Gooseneck trailers allow an ordinary pickup truck to handle great weight while making it easier to turn in tight quarters.

duty three-quarter-ton pickup could do the same for two full-sized horses.

That said, the disadvantages loom large. First, a stock rack offers the animals no protection from wind or cold, so you'll probably want to put a tarp over it or at least rig a windbreak on the front. The second, more serious disadvantage has to do with the high center of gravity of full-sized horses and mules. Stand them on a pickup bed that is already thirty inches higher than the ground, and the loaded truck's center of gravity rises dramatically—as much as a couple of feet. That situation is worsened by the animals constantly shifting their weight, which cannot be compensated for by tying them. Every movement shifts the vehicle on its springs, which, coupled with the normal motion of driving, can produce a ship-at-sea effect that should be avoided. Even if you do not get motion sickness, think of what the animals are going through. To keep the experience safe and humane, the driver must do everything— braking, acceleration, turning, and especially stopping—more slowly and gradually than normal. The whole trip is likely to be a little unnerving for the uninitiated.

The stock rack approach poses other difficulties, too. Since the pickup bed is occupied, you cannot haul your other gear there. Unless your animals are trained to jump into and out of the pickup bed, you'll need a loading ramp, and not all trailheads have them. When I bought my old Tennessee walker mare, Mona, I didn't own a trailer, but I did have an old pickup with a stock rack that I used occasionally to haul a cow to market. After finalizing the deal to buy Mona over the telephone, I went to the outfitter's place to pick her up in my truck. I didn't see any sort of loading chute and started wondering if the outfitter maybe used a ditch bank; that method often serves the purpose, but it can be hazardous. I had agreed to spend about all could afford for the horse, and I didn't like the idea of her getting injured before I even

got her home. What I didn't know is that this outfitter hauled all his horses and mules in truck beds, and he trained them to load without a ramp.

At sixteen hands two inches, Mona is a big mare. She weighs about 1,200 pounds and at that time was even bigger because she was ten and a half months pregnant. A little girl brought her to me, and I asked the outfitter if he had a ramp. "Don't need one," he said. "Open 'er up."

His confidence did little to soothe my concerns for all this horse flesh, but I raised the sliding rear gate on the stock truck, realizing he intended to load her without a ramp. I looked at the huge sorrel, looked at my truck, and shook my head. He parked Mona behind the pickup, tossed her lead rope through the end gate, and gave the command: "Jump, Mona." And she did! When her front feet came down in the middle of the pickup bed the old truck squatted visibly; it dipped further when her hind legs hopped into place. The pickup sat there quivering, but Mona seemed content, and I remember thinking she was really worth several hundred dollars more than I had paid.

I know of only one man who uses his pack animals often and has stuck with the stock rack method because he is entirely happy with it. A barber by trade, this man is short and muscular, and he has discovered what many do not know: Horses do not have to be large to get the job done. He owns two small ones, including an American walking pony (walker/Welsh cross) gelding. Because his horses are small, they fit easily in the box of his pickup even though it has a large tool chest across the front. He has carpeted the tool box for padding and built a windbreak around the front portion of the stock rack. On longer trips, when he wants a nice camp at the trailhead, he hitches a small camping trailer to the back of his outfit. He has fun with his horses and goes on many trips, so I assume the arrangement has worked out very well.

For most people, however, a good horse trailer is a more satisfactory piece of gear than a stock rack. Trailers come in so many sizes, shapes, and capacities that a first-time buyer is likely to be overwhelmed. If your pack animals are ponies, burros, or llamas, you can incline toward lighter-capacity units, though I have noticed that llama breeders often use four-horse combination stock trailers.

If you don't own a pickup truck, look for a two-horse trailer designed to be pulled by a passenger car. Automobile manufacturers' recommendations on towing capacity, both for total trailer weight and for hitch weight, generally can be trusted, since they tend to be conservative.

Two-horse trailers are practical if you're going light on horseback or if you plan to hike with a pack-animal assist. Most such trailers have a lockable tack compartment in front, which is handy because it leaves the bed of the towing vehicle uncluttered. The majority also have a feed bunk in front and some sort of lengthwise divider between the two horse stalls. Since this divider is removable, some of the wider models might accommodate three llamas or other small pack animals. A loaded two-horse trailer is normally still light enough to be towed by a half-ton pickup or a full-sized sport-utility vehicle. It is no longer uncommon to see the smaller sport-utility vehicles and imported pickups pulling such trailers, partly because

Our 1949 cattle truck effortlessly handles three geldings, and it could carry two more if loaded side-to-side, tails and heads alternating.

these classes of vehicles have become larger and more powerful in recent years.

What should you look for in a trailer? Here are some of my biases. Tack compartments should open on each side of the trailer, not just on the right. This is an option you can do without, but you won't regret paying for it. Adequate height inside is also important. My trailer is only seventy-eight inches high inside and an inch shorter under the roof braces. It's just not big enough for the two tall geldings (more than 16 hands tall) I frequently haul. Of course, all the standard horse trailers are plenty high for llamas and ponies.

Trailer width also varies greatly. For many years five feet was standard, and that width is adequate. But a large horse often cannot turn around in a trailer five feet wide. Worse, many can, but just barely, and on that morning when everything else goes wrong a large horse sometimes tries and gets stuck—no fun for you or the horse. All horses should be taught to back out of trailers, but it is certainly useful to have enough width—six feet or more—to allow the animals to turn around.

Few trailers in my region have ramps on the back. The prevailing opinion seems to be that horses should be taught to step up as needed. It's a bit tougher to teach them to step down with their hind legs when backing out, but that can be accomplished with patience.

Electric brakes have become pretty standard. Some people still favor surge brakes, but I cannot agree. Surge brakes are activated by the change in momentum caused by applying the brakes on your tow vehicle. If you stop on an icy back road and have to hold the whole outfit in place on a grade, surge brakes cannot be applied. Electric brakes can be activated by moving a lever on the brake unit mounted under the dash of your tow vehicle.

There are a host of additional "nice-to-haves." For example, walk-in tack rooms are wonderful. Some are large enough that you can roll out a sleeping bag in an emergency.

Many horse trailers can be completely enclosed, which is particularly handy in some climates. Many stock trailer owners (myself included) in northern climates own insulated horse blankets that protect horses well when traveling in cold weather. But since excessive heat is more likely to prove deadly than excessive cold, make sure your trailer has adequate venting.

Slant-load trailers seem to be growing in popularity, though they evoke considerable differences in opinion on them. In theory, the horses ride better, since the angle of the trailer braces them against both side-to-side and front-to-back motion. Some owners complain that loading and unloading are more difficult in slant-load trailers. The trailer itself must be larger: slant load three-horse trailers are approximately equal in size to conventional four-horse models.

Four-horse trailers are at the upper size limit of bumper-pull types. When pulling them it's well to consider an Equalizer or other frame-mounted hitch rather than a bumper hitch. For larger trailers the gooseneck (fifth wheel) configuration begins to make a great deal of sense; even two- and four-horse goosenecks are becoming quite popular. Gooseneck models offer two main advantages. First, the hitch weight is over the rear wheels of the truck where it belongs, not back on the bumper where it tends to force the front of your truck upward. Second, since the hitch can swing in a wide arc goosenecks can be maneuvered so the trailer is angling back from the truck at ninety degrees or more to the side. A skilled driver can get such a trailer into tight trailheads inaccessible to a bumper trailer of a similar length.

There are also disadvantages. Gooseneck trailers can, obviously, only be pulled by pickup trucks, not by enclosed sport/utility vehicles. The hitch takes up most of the truck bed, although a tool box or single-bed sleeper (popular among rodeo folks in our state) can be fitted ahead of the hitch. The tack rooms in gooseneck trailers are normally in the front overhang, above the hitch. They are a bit difficult to access and require lots of lifting to load your gear. However, the overhang can also be used as emergency sleeping quarters.

The stock truck still has many advantages, but it is highly unlikely readers of this book will want to own one. We have one only because it was part of the deal when we bought the family ranch. Purchased new in 1949 by Emily's dad, the truck has a two-speed axle that makes its small six-cylinder engine able to lug a heavy load up a steep hill, assuming you're not trying to win any races. Even with its relatively short (thirteen-foot) bed, the truck's full eight-foot width accommodates three horses abreast. Loaded laterally, head to tail, such a truck will handle up to five full-sized horses; its heavy rear axle and dual tires are designed for such a load. Unloading is not a problem in our region because stock trucks were popular before horse trailers, and major Forest Service trailheads have ramps. Rural folks who do not already own pickup trucks might do well to consider a solid used stock truck as an all-around chore machine.

With trailers, too, buying a good used one may be a viable option, but be careful. The number one worry with trailers is rotten floors that might allow a horse's foot to drop through a hole onto the pavement. Lastly, if you are new to the whole business of transporting livestock, start slowly. Get used to pulling a load and practice the changes in driving required. Don't tackle a trip across the state for your first outing; go instead to a closer destination, unload your animals, rest, reload them, and come home. As with all seemingly mundane activities, there are skills involved, and they will come with practice.

What we're all looking for.

Treading Lightly with Pack Animals

7

A Family on the Trail

Wound up in low-range second gear, the 1949 cattle truck tackles the grade like an ancient trooper. I look in its one remaining mirror to see that my sons David and Steve, and my wife, Emily, are following close behind with pickup and trailer. The muffler of my truck is merely a memory, but the truck is nonetheless a jewel, built when they used armor plate for doors. With only 40,000 actual miles on the odometer and most of her years under a shed roof, the truck was ready and willing to transport three big geldings from our ranch to the trailhead.

We are five on this trip, a magic number because that's all of us—Mom, Dad, and their three boys (Jonathan rides with me in the truck) on a pack trip for the whole family. When your oldest child is twenty-two and college, jobs, and fate have entered in, you're

thankful for rare chances like this. So, although I tell myself repeatedly that short trips aren't worth the days of preparation, although it's just as much work to prepare for a two-night pack trip like this one as it is for a two-weeker, and although we'd scaled back our aspirations two or three different times, we are still glad to be toiling up the grade in two vehicles and glad for the chance to share the trail, the campfire, even the work.

With five people and seven horses we are certainly pushing the limits of "going it light." We economized on gear, but we are still past the load limit for a single pack horse. We need one fully loaded horse carrying two seventy-five pound manties and a second horse, two-thirds loaded, with panniers weighing forty-five pounds each. Since the less heavily

97

At a typical trailhead anticipation runs high.

loaded animal is a three-year-old not yet ready for heavy work, this works out well. Also, our packhorse-to-person ratio of 1 to 2.5 is a bit better than the sought-after 1 to 2.

Anticipation is the ruling emotion as our vehicles nosed toward the blue Beartooth Mountains, but I have to admit the anticipation is a tad on the weary side. Getting ready for a self-outfitted pack trip is a great deal of work. Gear not used for a year must be found, inventoried, and repaired. Since this was the largest group we had taken, some gear had to be bought. The horses we had not been using needed shoeing; the others needed a reset. Two vehicles and a horse trailer had to be checked out. These tasks, interspersed with our normally frantic summer ranch

work, left me feeling I *needed* the mountains.

We used both of the pack methods outlined earlier in this book. Star Wars, one of our best Tennessee walking horse brood mares, carries a Decker pack saddle and two large manties made up around plywood pack boxes. Sweetness personified (except toward other mares), the big black mare has not been used for eight years, but I don't fear any problems. I did take the sensible precaution of saddling her up a couple days before the trip, securing two mantied hay bales in a basket hitch, and leading her on a conditioning run to the hills. She accepted all that as if she'd packed in last week.

Marshmallow, a gelding so colorful you'd have to call him loud, carries our other load.

Also a Tennessee walker, Marshmallow is the heavy-boned type. Three years old and not yet saddle broke, this gelding had packed on one other trip that spring, and most of his youthful kinks have been ironed out. He carries a sawbuck saddle and two nylon panniers. With two horses we have plenty of capacity, so no top pack is needed.

I like to prepare the first day's loads at home so they're ready to put on the pack horses at the trailhead. I get nervous at trailheads. I'm anxious for the transition to the trail, but also, I think, I've been the "responsible one" so long—the officer when I was a marine, the boss, the dad, the one who would have the most to feel guilty about if something went wrong. It's a morbid outlook, I know, so I try not to indulge in it very much. One of its primary symptoms is the nagging question, "What have I forgotten?" "Is the first-aid kit really in my saddle bags?" "Are the embarrassing essentials—can opener, matches, toilet paper—along?" My ability to overcome this anxiety is directly related to the time I spend preparing a good list before assembling the gear.

Assembling the packs at home lets me be a little more deliberate, a little more careful. As a result, the woodstove area of our living room was taken over for several days

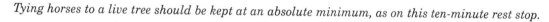

Tying horses to a live tree should be kept at an absolute minimum, as on this ten-minute rest stop.

by manty tarps, panniers, and a goodly assortment of gear. Into the plywood pack boxes went all the hard stuff: stove, camp stools, canned goods. Into the panniers went two backpacking tents, several sleeping bags, and pads. The panniers, so much more accessible than the manties, also hold anything that might be needed quickly. During packing I'm constantly lifting the box or pannier. I've become reasonably good at detecting whether loads for each side of the pack animal are of equal weight. What works best for me is to lift, then do a full curl with the load, flexing my arms and raising the item to my chin. Using muscular memory, I move to the second load and repeat. I can usually detect a difference of more than a pound or two.

Not owning a proper scale for the purpose, I used the one from our bathroom. By putting two lengths of two-by-six board on edge on either side of the dial I created a platform on which to set the load. A shaving mirror held by the dial reflected the weight so I could read it. There is something satisfying about hitting the trail the first day with packs you know are equal.

We packed the panniers with our usual attention to the horse's comfort, keeping soft items on the inside. With the pack boxes to be mantied, we mainly concentrated on keeping the center of gravity a little below the midpoint of each. Boxes are unyielding, true, but the Decker saddle has several features that make this more bearable to the horse. A large pack pad underneath the saddle is the first line of defense. On top of this is the "half-breed," stuffed with horsehair. The third line of defense is presented by the fore-and-aft boards mounted inside the half-breed. These boards distribute the weight of the load, keeping it from digging into one place.

Once the hard items were loaded inside the boxes we placed softer items on top to pad the load and give the manty ropes something to compress. Then it was out to the lawn,

where David and I mantied the loads. All this was new to David: Although he is a dedicated backpacker and did a reasonable amount of riding while he was growing up, he had never packed on horses with me. But he learned the mantying process quickly and found an application for it later that summer, when he neatly mantied up a queen-sized mattress and box spring in a tight package that rode 800 miles on the boat bars of his pickup without slacking a line. That simple principle of a series of half-hitches, each increasing the effectiveness of the other, can have many applications.

There were other livingroom preparations, too. Every horse needed a lead rope, and I was about three short. I made up several of the strongest kind, with no snaps, by splicing an eye in one end of ten feet of half-inch nylon rope and back-splicing the other. You insert the eye through the loop on the halter and the end of the lead rope back through the eye. It takes a couple of seconds longer than attaching with a snap, but it's far stronger, and it's silent.

Now on the road, we head toward the west fork of the Stillwater River in south-central Montana. We are among that tiny percentage of lucky Americans who can drive to several wilderness trailheads in less than an hour. When I'm feeling cynical I would add that we work extremely hard for the privilege, accepting considerably less financial reward for what we do in exchange for living under the "Big Sky." But on good days the exchange is fair. The cynical local expression, "You can't eat scenery," does not come to mind as I stare at the Beartooths through the truck's cracked windshield.

Earlier in the summer we had planned a five-day, four-night trip. As the work snowballed one day was shaved off, then another. We decided we could manage three days and two nights under the stars, no more. So talk of crossing the high plateau and fishing the lakes changed to talk of a single pleasant two-night camp along the river in the upper portion of the valley. We would cut down on the work created by one-night camps and try to have more time to . . . well, whatever.

For the first half of the trip the road is paved; the second half is Forest Service "gravel" sifted through a screen with twelve-inch openings. The road climbs so steeply that I wonder if the old truck will have gears low enough. It does, but just barely. David, be-hind, has the pickup in low range. Jonathan and I, in the truck, try to converse over the roar and just about give up. Headed for Tulane University in New Orleans, Jon might be thinking about trips he will not take this fall, trips to hunt elk through the golden quaking aspen with his dad on horseback. But he is smart enough to know that the world stretches past our back pasture fence, smart and eager to try his legs at the school and in an ROTC unit. Maybe he'll grow to love Cajun

Emily.

101

country, exciting in itself. And I know he'll grow to love these mountains even more through being deprived of them for a few years. Another college boy comes to mind, one who went to Iowa, whose eyes came back empty each time he looked off from football practice at a horizon with no mountains.

We are lucky enough never to meet another rig on one of the narrow places, and soon the trailhead is there. Now I really begin to appreciate the muscles of three eager boys. First, the horses come out, three geldings from the truck. Rockytop Tennessee, age eleven, is the first colt I raised from a foal and trained, a sorrel capable of crankiness but always good in tough places. Rockytop was on the cover of the July 1990 *Equus* magazine, but was unimpressed by that when I showed it to him. Like Rockytop, Marauder is well over sixteen hands, black, and the ultimate gentleman. Ace is a hand shorter than his two buddies but even more athletic, a bit of a spitfire, and extremely smooth. Emily will ride him.

There are four horses in the trailer. Misty, a red-roan mare of three, is already well broke but in need of experience. She belongs to Steve, our fourteen-year-old, but brother Jon will ride her. Then there are Star Wars and Marshmallow, who will carry the packs, and Mona, at twenty-one much the oldest horse along but still healthy and steady for Steve. All seven are Tennessee walking horses, not the only good breed for the mountains but the one we raise, the breed whose good dispositions and fast smooth gaits have spoiled us.

There are no hitching rails at the trailhead, so tying to the trailer and trees was necessary. The saddling goes fast. We have not yet noticed the absence of any forgotten item, so my disposition is improved. We ready the saddle horses first, tying them by the halters with bridles on and reins up to the saddle horns where they're secured by two half hitches. We get our mounts completely ready, lacking only the last notch to be taken on the cinch, before we load the packhorses. The latter will carry their loads all day, so we must not make them stand loaded any longer than necessary. I heft the first manty up on Star Wars, secure it with a basket hitch, and ask Jon to lift up on it a little until I get the other in place. They go on just right the first time, and I'm delighted. Nestled into their sling ropes the packs rest with their tops dead level with each other. We know from the scale that one is about a pound heavier, so we put the shovel through the manty ropes of that one and the heavier ax on the other side.

Loading Marshmallow might be touchier. Although a very gentle colt, he developed an aversion to being packed on his right side last spring on the bear hunt. He has gradually gotten over it, but I still rest the pannier on his shoulder first, lean it there a moment, then slide it gradually toward its proper position. I lift it high enough, then David helps from the other side by placing the looped straps over the sawbuck. When he gives me the word, I lower it.

Once the horses are loaded and ready, I've always felt it is best to get going quickly. It seems that the quicker you can get on the trail, the less potential there is for a wreck. We make a last check of the doors of the vehicles, a last look around at the ground for the saddlebag that didn't get loaded, a last feel under each cinch. Then we swing ourselves up into the saddles and go.

Our original plan was for me to lead the two packhorses with the colt up front and the mare Star Wars pigtailed to him. But putting him behind her would have likely gotten him kicked, and we discovered on our little exploratory trip to the hills that it worked extremely well for me to lead the colt while David took the big mare. So now I lead the way on the big black, Marauder. With larger strings it is better for a horseman unencumbered with pack animals to lead the party, followed by the person leading the string. Since he's a bit more footloose, this front rider can scout out obstacles and call a halt if the ax or saw (normally kept on the first packhorse) is needed. He can also warn the pack leader of an oncoming pack train. Today following Marauder and me are Marshmallow with the sawbuck, David on Rockytop leading Star Wars with the Decker, then Steve on old Mona, Emily on Ace, and Jonathan on the filly Misty.

The horses are primed to go and no spurs are necessary. Marauder leads in a brisk, flat-footed walk that would be a tad fast if an all-Tennessee walker string weren't behind him. The lodgepole pines on each side of the trail stream past as if on conveyer belts, and it's time for that first free breath, the one that says, "We're off! We're doing it!"

A few minutes up the trail we overtake a middle-aged man with a pack on his back. Beside him is a female lab, also carrying a pack. We exchange cheerful greetings. He's headed to a little-used alpine lake, the trail to which is a rumor only (it's not on the map); we stop for a minute to discuss the best way to find it. He compliments our horses and professes some envy of them, but I don't think he feels the slightest bit deprived. Nor should he: He's going it light and alone with a pack dog to help, and he leaves us feeling he'll find the lake if it takes him all summer.

The travel itself is uneventful but nice. I'm constantly asking David if the sawbucks on top of Marshmallow's saddle are staying centered, and he as frequently asks the brother behind him the same question about the D-rings of the Decker on Star Wars. We don't boast at first, but after a few miles without needing to touch the load of either pack horse, the packs staying centered and even, we begin to consider ourselves pretty good packers. We observe a rest stop of five or ten minutes each hour, getting off our horses and having a drink from our canteens, checking

cinches while we are off. Everything is the way it is supposed to be—a cooling breeze easing through the trees, the smell of pine, the family truly a unit and traveling to a new place to set up camp like families of old, of many past races and cultures, before civilization put us on pavement.

It is eight miles to our intended destination, Breakneck Park. That's just right, far enough to get into new country but not so far that the trail becomes tiresome or the body sore. Nearly a mile long, Breakneck is a curved park with a dandy campsite at each end. Its size and curved shape mean a horse party can camp in each end without either of them bothering, or seeing, the other. We are hoping for the camp at the lower end, and since it's Monday and early in the summer season, the beginning of that stretch when the high country is free enough of snow to allow access to the alpine lakes, we're confident the park will be empty. The trail is free of human footprints, and the only horse tracks look old.

Last year Emily, Steve, and I rode up this same trail following what I first thought was the track of a dirt bike. A bit indignant, I commented that dirt bikes are illegal in this wilderness area and that maybe we'd spot the perpetrator. As we progressed up the trail, however, even my limited tracking expertise detected a flaw in my theory. When a two-wheeled vehicle turns, the rear wheel cuts the corner on the path of the front one so two tracks are left, not one. This track went around sharp corners but stayed single. A mountain unicycle? Speculation among the three of us grew, and the mystery became more fun. Finally we reached what appeared to be a backpacker's camp nestled on a ledge above the river. Next to the blue tent was a long aluminum basket frame with a wheel in the center of it. Obviously the contraption was built for two packers who would rather push and pull their load than carry it, and it looked quite efficient.

On that trip I was riding Rockytop and he shied at the strange contraption, so I didn't stop to talk. Since then I've seen the rig advertised in the back of sporting magazines. If you could build a similar affair, but with shafts for a pony, you could have the laziest trip of all by walking and leading the pony, which could pull the load considerably easier than either of you could carry it. Such a plan, and that of the two campers we observed, would depend on the regulations of the wilderness area involved, however. All American wilderness areas prohibit the use of anything with an engine except in special circumstances, but their position is less uniform about things that have wheels but no engines. The mountain bike craze brought this issue to a head. Concern revolves around whether the tracks left by wheels help cause erosion and whether such machines fit the wilderness experience expected by others. I reflected on this as we rode past the innovative campers. Their wheeled platform, powered by their muscle and sweat, bothered me little, even if it did bother Rockytop. But a mountain bike, hurtling unexpectedly down the trail at our horses at thirty miles per hour, would have been a different story.

David cooks under a manty sun cover, enjoying our new "Rollatable."

As we near Breakneck Park there is a subtle change in our surroundings. This has been a good year for rain, so it's been green since the trailhead. But as we rise in elevation toward the peaks that catch even the little storms, the valley floor seems more lush. Maybe it's just my mood. The last few hectic days fade, and simpler realities take their place.

We cross several smaller parks, all usable camping areas with water nearby and good grass for the horses. These will provide alternatives should we find a party in each end of the big park. I holler back to ask Steve how he's doing. Steve is riding using my McClellan saddle. Many people think the old cavalry saddles are extremely comfortable, and I agree they can be, but mine is a replica built on a hard fiberglass tree. Further, playing with the buckle adjustment on the saddle leathers always seems necessary to keep the buckle from gouging the rider's leg. Apparently we've solved that problem, for Steve is comfortable.

We ford still another creek, but this one looks familiar, and we break out into the open. "We're here," I yell. There are shouts of approval from the rest of the clan. Ahead of us, to the south, is the long park with grass aplenty. To our left, a willow thicket marks

Emily gives Ace some TLC.

the course of the river; to our right is the timbered ridge that forms the west valley wall. On the south end is a wall of granite rising up to Breakneck Peak, where a snowfield melts out the summer. The park bends east in the middle, so we cannot see the other end of it, but we won't even check for another group there. We have our preferred campsite.

We tie up near, but not in, the camping area. We use large trees, but will do so only for a few minutes, just until we can get the packs down, saddles off, and hobbles and picket lines out from the left pannier. I've put them on top so they can be reached readily. We lead the two pack horses, one at a time, over to within fifty feet of our prospective kitchen area. That's close enough; we drop panniers and manties on that spot. We'll carry the pack boxes to the kitchen area and unload tents and such from the panniers on the spot. Later, we'll tidy it all up.

As quickly as we unload the horses we begin hobbling them and turning them onto the grass. This park is unusually secure when it comes to holding horses. Our camp will be on the lower end, right next to the trail. Horses do not have an infallible sense of direction, but they have a good one, and if they should decide to return home they'll know enough to head down, not up. I've camped here before and know I can secure one reliable horse by tying him for the night. The rest I will leave hobbled, taking the precaution of stringing a lariat rope across the trail where it enters the timber between two big trees. But I will not do this until dark, in case someone should pass this way. Meanwhile, we'll watch the horses while we work. I had planned to set up an electric fence enclosure, as discussed in Chapter Four, but nature did not cooperate: Two days before we packed up a lightning storm toasted the tiny battery-operated charger.

David enjoys the hammock, which broke shortly after this picture was taken. Tree-savers should always be used.

The saddles all go into a neat pile, compact enough to be covered by a manty tarp. The bridles hang on a smooth, cooperative stub of branch that projects from a pine. We'll cover them also. The rest of the camp begins to take shape. The boys set up their backpacking tent; Emily and I set up ours. The kitchen evolves under a triangle of pines just right for holding shock cord strung out to the grommets I'd installed in the corners of the manty tarps. Soon we have a "roofed" kitchen, under which we set up a new luxury, a roll-up table made of slats enclosed in vinyl. On it goes the two-burner stove, and under it the plywood pack boxes that serve as portable kitchen cabinets.

Inside the tents we make our beds, unstuffing our sleeping bags and rolling them out onto their pads. They'll fluff and be all the warmer if they have some time out of their stuff sacks. Then we gather firewood. Not far into the woods we find downed, dead trees. Were this a fall hunting camp needing much wood I'd drag these dead trees in with a lariat dallied around the saddle horn. But our fire will be recreational only. This campsite has a semipermanent fireplace of large rocks, the kind we no longer like to make because of the blackened rocks it leaves. Since this site is heavily used by outfitters, the Forest Service has decided it's better to allow such a fireplace rather than requiring a separate firepit for every party. Even so, I'm so trained to use the low-impact type that I have twinges of conscience in making the fire here.

With camp set up and the horses eating, we rest a while. We've brought folding camp stools, the wood-framed type, which neatly fit the pack boxes and allow items to be placed inside their frames. We get them out and enjoy them. I've packed two dozen eggs inside the stools with softer stuff packed around them, and I check them triumphantly. Not one is broken. (I've given up, by the way, on the plastic egg holders sold in backpacking

stores. I use the original foam cartons with layers of folded paper towel inside to take up the slack, tape them closed, then enclose them in a plastic bag.)

Soon the sun disappears over the west mountain wall, and the temperature drops with it. The boys build up the fire, and we eat hamburgers and corn. We steal a little from our small stash of beer and soft drinks, which the boys have hemmed into a little pool in the small brook that passes the camp on its way to the river. The drinks have stayed very cold. We tell stories by the fire and speculate about the stars. The younger boys are optimistic about the possibility of life somewhere up there. David, who has taken college-level astronomy, tries to convey a more pessimistic view, but to no avail. Once each hour I check the horses, for they've grazed south over a knoll, and I cannot always see or hear them. Just before bed, I pick two dominant ones and picket them. Then I put the lariat rope across the trail in the preselected spot.

Once in bed I lie listening for the horses, dozing and waking, each time not satisfied until I hear a pair of hobbled hooves strike or a horse's mouth munch grass. How many men in history have lain half asleep in their lodges, listening for their horses? Indians would sometimes tie a favorite pony short near the teepee, then run a thong from the horse down under the edge of the lodge wall and tie it to their wrist so they would be awakened if someone tried to steal the horse. But I must be quite confident in our setup, for I am soon sound asleep.

Then next morning I awake first. Emily is a light sleeper, but her new compact cot and warmer sleeping bag have agreed with her. It is barely light enough to read my watch, but I feel rested and also slightly anxious about the horses. I rise to a standing, humped-over position. The Eureka! four-man tent has been a very good one, for I bought it nearly twenty years ago. But it's easy to understand the attraction of the peaked range tents that are so popular among packers for light camps: You can stand up in them. Pulling jeans on while humped over is an exercise for a younger man (or one in better shape), I decide, and I make plans for a new tent next summer.

The horses are fine, and I almost feel guilty about expecting the worst from them. They've stayed together, and they seem delighted at my visit. I pet each. Marshmallow is not used to hobbling, so he's been rough on himself. His pasterns are chafed. I tie him, and when I rehobble him I'll swipe some soft leather hobbles off Marauder to replace the nylon ones the younger horse has been wearing. Marauder is so adept at hobbling he travels with his front feet together with complete ease, even slack in the strap between his feet. Mona, the old dominant mare, looks a little tired. I move her picket line to better feed, both to protect the ground and to help the horse, for at twenty-one she needs the best.

I pump the stove quietly. The two-burner compact model is a pretty good traveler, for when packing I can load it with canned goods, spare fuel bottles, you name it. I've taken a one-burner backpacking model along just in case, but never need it this trip. On lighter horse trips we've taken two backpacking stoves, a good system that allows a second burner when needed and a back-up the rest of the time.

Soon the coffee pot is perking. I watch the sun hit the top of Breakneck Mountain, turning the granite red on each side of the snowfield. We had a discussion last night on whether the mountain was named after the park, or vice versa. Also who, or what, broke a neck up there? Maybe the name's origin is unrelated to that. The park (and the valley) make an abrupt bend in the middle, and maybe that's where the name came from. There are no doubt oldtimers who know.

I sip the first sierra cup of black coffee. I glance away from the blooming peaks to the willow bottoms on my left and for the first time notice the moose. How long has it been there? I take it to be a cow and don't bother with the binoculars. Later, when the boys rise, it is still there, and we christen it Molly Moose until someone notices tiny antlers. Then he becomes Morris Moose. Our cat back home would be honored if he knew.

The sunlight has crept almost down to the timberline on the peak by the time I pour my second cup of coffee. It will be a fine day. I enjoy planning it so much I decide no one should ever camp only one night in one good spot if there is any way to avoid it. Too often, we civilized types drag our hectic daily schedules right along with us on the very trips we're taking to get away from them. How many pack trips, hunting trips, road trips, and boat trips have been ruined because of the "gotta get there" psychology? If we were moving today I would already be begrudging the rest of the family their pleasant sleep-in.

Just the same, it isn't long until they stir: Emily first, of course. Soon we have sausages frying, and I stir the fire back to life. We don't really need it, but it's a friend from last night whose acquaintance we want to renew. A more materialistic concern is that it will burn the paper plates so we don't have to pack them out.

The day, indeed, turns out to be a good one. The boys fish a little and throw the frisbee a lot. Emily and I take a difficult hike up a trail on the west valley wall, up to where the air is thin. We crouch down while a mule deer buck with velvet antlers grazes his way toward us, closer, closer, until I take his picture and the self-winding shutter moves him away.

When we get back to camp we target practice with the .22 revolver we've brought. Were someone camped in the other end of the park I'd defer to their sense of peace and pass on this recreation, but in this setting it is harmless and fun. Emily decides the horses need some TLC, so she takes the curry comb and goes from one to another, petting, currying, and rubbing all over. Each horse greets her as a treasured guest. The comb gently scratches their insect bites, and they sway with it.

Today we see other people. A man and his daughter from back East walk into camp and tell us they've been brought to a camp below us by an outfitter who will pick them up today. The outfitter's base camp is in the Boulder drainage west of us, and he has brought them over the extremely steep west ridge. They confess to having had some real misgivings when the mules headed down the slope.

Two hours later the outfitter's string of solid, fast-walking mules comes past our camp. We put lead ropes on our nosiest horses to keep them out of the string's way. The outfitter and his guides appreciate this and say thanks. They'll be going down to have lunch with their paying guests, then pick them up and head back over the mountain.

Later that afternoon, a string comes down from the high country. They were the first party this summer to get into a particular lake, and they plowed through snow chest-deep on their horses to get there. The fishing, they say, was worth it. Toward evening still another string appears, this one from below. They ask if anyone is camped on the upper end of the park, and we tell them

Emily with Ace, the horse that needed to go up the mountain, not down.

109

no. They ride on, and an hour later we see the first of their released pack horses grazing down into view about a half-mile above us.

Two hours later, around supper time, we experience some excitement. A half-dozen of our neighbor's horses have been grazing our way, but they've been behaving themselves, so we aren't worried. Now and then we hear the pleasant tinkle of the bell the big bay mare is wearing. Suddenly we see our horses fling their heads upward, look up-country, and snort. I half expect a herd of elk but instead see the outfitter's horses stampeding straight toward us. Our own horses are loading up, getting ready to join the fun and, if necessary, gallop all the way to the trailhead. Jon and I pick up lead ropes in midstride. I grab the two most likely participants, Rockytop and Ace, and yell for Jon to catch the neighbor's bell mare. Luckily, she's cooperative. Even then, no one will settle down. Rockytop is so excited he's hard to hold, even hobbled, so I work him over to a tree and tie him tight.

In the Marine Corps we often had immediate action drills, with no advance warning, to test our ability to react to a new situation. The wrangler from the neighboring camp has just had his, and he passes admirably. In seconds we spot him, yellow slicker bouncing up and down behind the saddle on his galloping horse, running flat-out toward us. He only eases up a little when he sees Jon has caught the mare. He substitutes his lead rope for ours, and thanks us profusely. "She thought there was cake down here, I guess," he says. We gather this outfitter has often used the camp we are in, but on the way through was too decent to say so. He did not want us to feel we were cramping his operation in any way.

Evening comes, and with it another fire and more good talk. We polish off the rest of our beer and pop. The night chills enough to make the fire feel good, so hot chocolate is the next round.

The next morning we move briskly, but not hurriedly, to break camp. Since we are going home, we are not worried about whether we'll get to our next chosen campground first. At the same time, we want to be on the trail relatively early, before it gets hot.

We strike the tents and begin to pack. I place the pack boxes and panniers in an open, level area and ask the rest of the family to bring me everything that goes in them. Soon David takes over preparing the panniers. We enjoy packing the lighter loads: So much is always gone when we head back out. Paper towels and paper plates have been used and burned; cans of all kinds have been emptied of their heavy contents, rinsed with water, and smashed; and eggs and other fragile items are gone. The garbage sack is relatively light, and we put a second bag over the first.

Before we seal up the garbage sack, we perform the most important single act of low-impact camping. We get on line and do a thorough policing of the area, picking up everything non-organic. Even before building our first fire we went through the old ashes and picked out bits of aluminum foil. Now, the fire doused, we look for more. We remove bits of line we've tied to the trees.

At the edges of the camp area we scatter horse droppings, some from our animals, some older. The end result is pleasing: If the camp area has suffered from our presence, we can't detect it.

The packs, now lighter, load onto the pack saddles more easily. But the saddle horses know they are going home, and they're snorty. Emily mounts Ace, the most spirited. He does nothing wrong, but she can feel the energy radiating from him and says, "He shouldn't be going home. He should be going straight to the top of that peak, then down and up again." It's just heart, I guess, the kind coupled with excess energy, the kind that can be a problem but can also get you where you want to go come hell or high water.

We share the horses' mood. The trip has been fine, and if we were planning three more days we'd be looking forward to each. But the plan is to head out, and once that decision is made we're as spirited as the horses. The walk out is fast, sometimes too fast, and I have to rein Marauder in to remind him he's leading a pack horse with less mobility than he has. On the more level areas the whole string hits a running walk. The family doesn't even care to rest; we cover the eight miles of rocky trail in well under two hours, and it seems even faster. Then we're at the trailhead, eyeballing the trucks for damage or vandalism. (It's a sad fact that there is a certain type of thief who specializes in unattended vehicles at remote trailheads.)

But all is well. A middle-aged couple drives up in a pickup and greets us. They are people who have visited our ranch, who own horses but do not use them much, and who think about trips but do not take them. They admire our horses and pet them.

We do not feel zapped until we get into the vehicles, and then we are very tired and thirsty. I stop at Nye to get us all a coke. I think we get so tired after these trips, on the road out, because the trip itself is not there to be looked forward to anymore. But that is easily remedied. All it takes is to begin planning the next one. And we do. Next summer, yes, we'll take the long one, over the plateau, past the lakes, down the next drainage. Who knows? Maybe everyone's plans will work out, and we can all go together again.

Appendix A: Where to Go: Some Contacts

1. The Forest Service, under authority of the U.S. Department of Agriculture, is steward of much of the most desirable backcountry. Call them at (202) 447-3957 for "A Guide to your National Forests," which lists regional offices to contact for more detailed information on the area that interests you.

2. The Bureau of Land Management (BLM), under authority of the U.S. Department of the Interior, controls most of the federally owned lands that are not part of the national forests, and these lands, too, are open to public recreation. For information on recreational opportunities and the addresses of regional offices, contact:

BLM Public Affairs Office
Interior Bldg.
18th and C St., NW
Washington, DC 20240
(202) 343-5717

3. Backcountry Horsemen of America (P.O. Box 597, Columbia Falls, MT 59912) is an extremely helpful, fast-growing organization that stresses conservation through, among other things, volunteer trail maintenance work (usually in conjunction with the Forest Service) and education. It works to protect access by equine fanciers to the many public trails occasionally jeopardized by legislation. This organization has pro-

duced several fine pamphlets such as "Mountain Manners," free for the asking. Consider working with other horse people of backcountry orientation to start a chapter of this excellent group in your own vicinity. As of this writing, eight state chapters have been formed in addition to local divisions. The state chapter addresses are:

BCH of California
P.O. Box 520
Springville, CA 93265

BCH of Idaho
P.O. Box 513
Salmon, ID 83467

BCH of Montana
P.O. Box 5431
Helena, MT 59604

BCH of Nevada
P.O. Box 2202
Carson City, NV 89721

BCH of Washington
P.O. Box 563
Leavenworth, WA 98826

BCH of Wyoming, Wind River Chapter
P.O. Box 1137
Riverton, WY 82501

BCH of New Mexico, Pecos Chapter
P.O. Box 1095
Edgewood, NM 87015

BCH of Oregon,
Blue Mountain Chapter
P.O. Box 3022
LaGrande, OR 97850

4. The United States Geological Survey (under the Department of the Interior) publishes the nation's greatest collection of topographical maps. For areas east of the Mississippi River, contact:

Distribution Section,
U.S. Geological Survey
1200 South Eads Street
Arlington, VA 22202

For areas west of the Mississippi River, contact:

Distribution Section,
U.S. Geological Survey
Federal Center
Denver, CO 80225

You'll first want their index map for your destination state. This is a map of the whole state divided into grids labeled with the names of the large-scale maps available. From this you then order the individual maps.

Some sporting goods stores specialize in rather expensive (but nice) colorized versions of these maps, often printed on heavy, water-proof material.

Appendix B: Some Suppliers and Manufacturers

There are literally hundreds of suppliers of quality outdoor and packing gear. Listed below are some of which I have some personal knowledge. The ad sections of horse, hunting/fishing, and backpacking magazines will list many more.

Horse Packing Equipment/Wall Tents

Walker's Pack Saddlery
68633 Allen Canyon Loop (B)
Wallowa, OR 97885
(800) 253-5841/(503) 569-2226
(This company features pole sets for wall tents that break down to packable size)

Montana Canvas Wall Tents
P.O. Box 390
Belgrade, MT 59714
(406) 388-1225
(Features light synthetic tents as well as canvas models)

Beckel Canvas Products
2232 S.E. Clinton
Portland, OR 97202
(503) 232-3362
(Specializes in "lightweight, low-impact camping equipment")

Reliable Tent and Awning Co.
P.O. Box 1271
Billings, MT 59101
(800) 544-1039

Backpacking and General Outdoors

Recreational Equipment, Inc.
Box 88125
Seattle, WA 98138
(Longtime supplier of excellent gear, this company's catalog gives excellent comparisons of gear specifications)

Gander Mountain, Inc.
Box 248, Hwy W
Wilmot, WI 53192
(General Outdoor)

Cabela's
812 13th Ave.
Sidney, NE 69160
(General Outdoor)

Pack Goats

Rocky Mountain Pack Goats
P.O. Box 772
Santaquin, UT 84655
(801) 754-5415
(Sells pack gear, trained goats, instructions packages, and also rents pack goats)

Miscellaneous

Picket Line Loop Rollin Beauchane
29600 S. Dryland Rd.
Canby, OR 97013
(503) 651-3690
(Sells the handy piece of hardware that can eliminate picket line loops)

Appendix C: Suggested Gear List

You probably don't need to take *all* the items listed below, but neither should you take *only* items from this list. Use the groupings as reminders to jar your memory and as seed stock for drawing up your own personalized list. If you have a home computer, keep a running list on it and adapt it periodically to changes in your taste, circumstances, age, etc.

Shelter and Sleeping

1. One good sleeping bag per person.

2. One sleeping pad, air mattress, or (extra-light) cot per person.

3. Tent (rated for one more person than is actually along; for example, bring a four-man tent for three people).

4. Ground cloth (if your tent has no floor). Manty tarp can be used.

5. Tarps for covering saddles and for rigging shelter over cook area. Manty tarps may serve double-duty.

6. Plenty of nylon cord and shock (bungee) cord for camp organization. Manty ropes work well.

For Pack Dogs

1. Packs.

2. Stout collar.

3. Light chain for restraint in camp.

4. Small food dish.

5. Dog food (possibly supplemented by "table" scraps); where legal and ecologically sound, fish and small game can contribute to the dog's diet.

6. Animal first-aid kit (your vet's recommendation).

For Horses, Mules, and Ponies

1. Pack saddle or riding saddle for each and pad.

2. One halter per animal (which they'll probably wear).

3. One lead rope each.

4. For each pack animal, a set of panniers or manty tarps and ropes along with sling ropes.

5. For each saddle animal, a set of saddle bags and/or horn pouches or cantle pack (so each rider can carry personal items).

6. One bridle for each saddle animal.

7. One restraint system per animal—that is, your total number of hobbles and picket-rope/hobble-half combinations should equal the number of animals, even if you plan a high picket line (you might camp where there are no trees). I prefer the electric corral to the picket line but still need the hobbles and picket ropes.

115

8. Hoof pick.

9. Curry comb.

10. Shoeing kit (fence pliers, horseshoe nails, other items your farrier suggests).

11. Optional and expensive but excellent—one or more pre-fitted Easyboots to replace lost shoes (take the most common sizes).

12. Equine first-aid kit. (Ask your vet. We take wound salve, iodine, sutures to close something really nasty, and both gauze and ace bandages. But you'll need to adjust as anticipated. The more animals and the longer the trip the more extensive the kit should be.)

13. Leather repair kit (punch and lacing material, at least).

14. Fly spray (some of the salves are good also, and some packers like the fly tags that attach to halters).

15. Feed (according to regulations and environment. Certified weed-free hay and pellets or rolled grain as needed).

16. Documentation. (In Montana all strangers are apparently still considered incipient rustlers, so brand inspections are required for crossing county lines, even if the horse isn't branded. In some states health certificates or negative Coggins tests are required. Usually such paperwork can be left in your vehicle at the trailhead.)

Camp Equipment

(This is the most subjective category, so adjust according to the relative lightness to which you aspire; the size, ages, and needs of your party; and the length of your trip.)

1. Ax (a real one, such as the cruiser type; not a hatchet. Hatchets are knee splitters because of the short arc of the one-handed swing, thus they are definitely more dangerous than an ax, especially for kids. Consider any ax fully as dangerous as a firearm, and keep it off-limits to the untrained. The ax head should be covered when not in use by a good leather sheath.)

2. File (for sharpening ax and shovel).

3. Folding saw (for firewood).

4. Folding canvas bucket.

5. Shovel (portable but capable).

6. Folding table or materials to rig a cooking surface.

7. Cooking stove (backpacker types for light trips, working up with size of party, length of trip, and time of year).

8. Lantern (candle or portable gasoline type with extra mantles).

9. Cookware. (On solo trips I get along with a sierra cup, a two-pound coffee can that doubles when packed as a stove container, and a small frying pan with folding handle. On family outings we use a medium saucepan, a large frying pan with folding handle, a coffee pot, and a coffee can for heating water. These items will cook almost everything.)

10. Cooking utensils (spatula, long fork, sheath knife, etc.).

11. Silverware (army surplus sets of fork, knife, and spoon, which clip together, work well.)

12. Dishes. (Paper plates cut down on dishwashing and burn in the fire, as do paper cups and bowls.)

13. Paper towels (plenty, because they are so handy).

14. Plastic trash bags (the tougher the better).

15. Toilet paper (flattened and kept dry in a resealable plastic bag).

16. Matches (including a reserve supply in a waterproof container).

17. Disposable propane lighters (better for starting fires than matches).

18. Fire-starting paste.

19. Can opener.

20. Extra generators for any Coleman or similar appliances plus a small wrench to change them.

21. Coleman fuel.

22. Sewing kit.

23. Biodegradable liquid soap.

24. Small whetstone.

Food

(These are only ideas and a few guidelines. Your diet may be vegetarian or kosher or something else that renders these suggestions ridiculous.)

1. Freeze-dried foods. (Outstanding for super-light trips, but quite expensive for longer trips with larger parties. Other dehydrated foods—such as Lipton dinners, soups, noodles, hot chocolate, hot cereal—are as good and much cheaper.)

2. Frozen meat. (Not too much; the trick is to package it in leak-proof bags and pack it in the excellent insulation supplied by your sleeping bag. Obviously, you must eat it during the early part of your trip.)

3. Canned goods. (Go easy on these; they're heavy, hard, and you must pack out the empty cans. But with large pack animals, there's room for some canned items. They're good for sandwich makings during the latter part of your trip.)

4. Bread. (It might get smashed but still tastes okay. Consider pan breads you can bake underway or a fold-flat oven to put on your stove.)

5. Eggs. (These keep quite well and aren't that difficult to pack. I've given up on the plastic backpacking containers; foam store cartons work better. I pack paper towels on both sides of the eggs, close the cartons, and tape them with masking or duct tape. Usually I don't lose any, and the foam container has some insulation value. Remember, though, to never burn styrofoam. Always pack it out.)

6. Margarine (lasts better than butter and is available in plastic squeeze bottles. You can use it for frying also, instead of cooking oil.)

7. Cheese spreads (squeeze-type or pressurized containers; good for sandwiches, cracker snacks, cheeseburgers.)

8. Beverages. (Take pop and beer in cans only, not bottles. You won't have room for much, if any. Presweetened powders, such as Kool Aid and Tang, are handier; just add water. Powdered milk is good if mixed and chilled well before serving.)

9. Water purifiers. (Tablets work fine but add taste; space-age filtration systems that filter out even Giardia are better.)

10. Meal plans. (Write these on paper for every meal of the trip before you leave, then buy what you need and organize each meal in a giant Ziplock bag; use a felt-tip pen to label each with the day and the meal.)

11. Pack at least one extra day of food for everybody. Two is better. You might decide to stay longer, and people eat more when living outdoors. Even in fine fishing country, don't count on fish as a major part of your diet. If you do, they won't bite.

12. Condiments. (Don't forget the salt, pepper, catsup, and mustard!)

Personal Items

1. Rain gear.

2. Warm clothing. (Wool is hard to beat; down vests feel good on chilly nights.)

3. Adequate changes of clothing, socks, and underwear, but keep it reasonable.

4. Hat (with enough brim to keep the sun and rain off).

5. Footwear. (On walking trips, waterproof yet breathable boots, such as those made of Gore-tex, are excellent. On riding trips a comfortable, broken-in pair of cowboy or packer boots is best. Tennis shoes wear well around camp.)

6. Medication (if you need it, bring plenty).

7. Fishing gear and license.

8. Camera and film. (The new-generation compact auto-focus 35mms are excellent, though their lenses are usually slightly wide angle, which makes mountains and wildlife appear farther away; zoom lenses correct this.)

9. Insect repellent (spray or cream, in small, personalized containers for carrying in pockets or in horn pouches on the saddle.)

10 Flashlight with extra bulb and batteries. (The small Maglite brand flashlights are excellent.)

11. Pocketknife.

12. Binoculars.

13. Sunglasses.

14. Toilet kit.

15. Leather gloves.

16. On horse trips, daypack or fanny pack for hikes away from the livestock.

Entertainment

Small books, a recorder or harmonica, Nerf or foam ball, Frisbee, playing cards—compact items to make life around the campfire and in the tent on a rainy day more enjoyable. If you consume alcohol, choose types that don't require mix and that transport in plastic or metal containers.

Safety

1. Maps of the area and a good orienteering compass, with the knowledge to use both.

2. First-aid kit. (Many fine ones available, but check them for completeness; don't assume.)

3. First-aid book (compact and thorough).

Appendix D: Horse and Pony Breeds

This quick overview is opinionated, even blunt, and is better skipped by any reader whose favorite breed is beyond criticism. If, however, some unabashed observations from a Montana mountain horseman are of interest, read on.

There are no "bad" horse breeds in the United States. All have evolved, naturally and with selective breeding, to be useful companions to mankind, and all are made up primarily of sound, capable animals. But horse conformation, like boat design, is a compromise, and not all breeds do all things equally well. Further, you can't be sure of always finding the same characteristics in a given breed. Most breeds have within them considerable variety. Worse, the proliferation of registration associations (now numbering in the hundreds) has made the situation even more confusing for the beginner. This appen-

Smooth and spirited under the saddle and tractable under the pack, Tennessee walking horses like Ace have become my favorites.

dix looks only at several of the best known breeds, and only briefly at that.

First, this is an area where it pays to be an individual. Evaluate your needs, look at the accomplishments of various breeds, and try to get to know some of the animals and their owners personally. Horse breeds, like dog breeds, have been very subject to the whims of fashion. If you are sixty and a novice rider, and you want a pleasure mount for yourself and your grandchildren, then you shouldn't be looking at hot-blooded horses with racing genes.

Second, consider whether a breed is popular in a given region because it really does the best job performing tasks common to that area. Or is its popularity the result of an aggressive public relations campaign or because it has become associated with an entrenched myth? Is the horse favored in that region because it was well suited to the tasks of yesteryear and its genes are still the most common ones available, even though the original purpose has faded?

Fashions and purposes change. For instance, invention of the horse trailer profoundly influenced the rise in popularity of some breeds, the fall of others. When horses had to cover extreme distances with a rider aboard, they were bred for smooth gaits (no one wanted a chop-chop trot for sixty miles) and endurance (usually meaning long muscles and a deep, but not wide, chest). Thus, in the days when people rode horses to horse shows or to mountain hunts or to cattle roundups, they viewed the necessary attributes quite differently than later days when they could haul horses to the events. Similarly, after the development of decent roads, many people quit riding because they preferred a comfortable buggy or wagon. This, again, de-emphasized smooth gaits. A trot in harness was not so rough for the passenger being pulled, so trotting was just fine.

Thus, areas of the world where poor roads persisted longest tend to be the ones we associate with "gaited" horse breeds, breeds with an intermediate gait (between the walk and the canter) that is smoother than the trot and usually four-beat. These "saddle" gaits, such as the running walk, the fox-trot, the amble, and the single-foot, occur naturally in equines but were brought out by selective breeding when a society had to stay on horseback late into its development and wanted comfort and endurance. In the southeastern United States, where roads were few and muddy (people took the steamboat when they could) such breeds as the Tennessee walking horse, the Missouri foxtrotter, and the naturally gaited saddlebreds gained favor. In Iceland a pony was bred that performed a "tolt," similar to a running walk. In Central and South America the various "paso" breeds developed, along with the Galiceno pony, all of which have smooth, fast, naturally four-beat gaits.

In areas where nongaited (trotting) horses prevail, there is sometimes an unfounded prejudice against gaited breeds by people who have little experience with them. Perhaps those folks have seen them only in the show ring and find it hard to believe the same horses could perform well in rough country. Actually, the reverse is true. The gaited breeds as a group are among the most surefooted, which is not surprising when you look at their backgrounds; they came from regions of the world where the going was tough. Some backcountry horsemen are concerned that, since other breeds often have trouble keeping up with gaited ones, a gaited saddle mount might move too rapidly to lead a pack-string. In practice, this is rarely a problem. Most gaited horses do like to move out, but most will throttle back as necessary. True, an all-walker or all-foxtrotter outfit, or

a gaited saddle mount leading a string of gaited mules (born to a jack sire and gaited mares), is perhaps the ultimate mountain machine, but gaited and nongaited animals can be compatible in one outfit.

Since I'll continue referring to gait in this discussion, some quick definitions are in order. A **walk** is a four-beat (each foot hits the ground at a different time) nonsuspension gait (three feet are on the ground at any given time). A **trot** is a two-beat suspension gait with the right front and left rear feet hit simultaneously, followed by the left front and right rear. The **pace** is also a two-beat gait, but the feet on one side of the horse hit simultaneously, followed by the two on the other side. The **canter** (also called the "lope" out west, the gallop when you speed it up) is technically a three-beat suspension gait; the horse springs off one hind foot, then the other hind and its diagonally opposed front simultaneously, followed by the other front. The **running walk**, **fox-trot**, **single-foot**, and **paso** gaits (performed by naturally gaited Latin American breeds) all are similar in speed to the trot, but much smoother. Like the walk, they are four-beat nonsuspension gaits. The "bumps" are divided into smaller pieces and the result is a smooth yet fast ride.

We'll start with my own favorite, the Tennessee walking horse. An all-American breed, the "walker" traces its heritage to Morgan, saddlebred, Thoroughbred, and standardbred lines, and probably also to the Canadian pacer. The walker's forebears were the workhorses of the American South, familiar with both harness and saddle, that took their owners to town with necks arched and heads up for the "doin's" on Saturday night. In the South, saddle horses had smooth gaits; otherwise, they were relegated to buggy duty. The breed solidified when a pacing standardbred stallion named Allan F-1 was bred to Tennessee native mares, and a remarkable percentage of the foals did a natural running walk—one of the sweetest things you'll ever feel under saddle. Gradually the breed grew and refined, and in 1935 the owners of these horses formed an association.

For backcountry travel and as a family horse, the walker has a great deal to offer. That assertion is substantiated by the fact that between 1980 and 1990 the walking horse was the only major breed that grew in registration and in transfer numbers; all other major breed associations declined during that decade. This growth (which continued beyond 1990) is especially remarkable when you consider that the walking horse received considerable unfavorable criticism during that period for some of the practices allegedly used in the training of "big lick" show horses. The breed association seems to be doing a good job of enforcing rather strict training regulations, so that black mark on the slate of a such a wonderful breed should be completely erased.

In any case, Tennessee walking horses, shod naturally (not with the thick pads used for some show events), are wonderful family horses. Their running walk is genetic, though they are multigaited. Most will trot or pace also, so the natural running walk can be refined and improved. Their smoothness is uncanny. I watched my wife ride one of our first walkers back and forth behind a high board fence. Her head and shoulders showed no up-and-down movement, as though she were on a conveyer belt. Ride a Tennessee walking horse with a friend mounted on a nongaited animal, and your friend will end up either wanting a walker or despising you. Before it even hits a running walk, your Tennessee walking horse will do a flat-footed walk so much longer and faster than a conventional walk that another breed would have to trot to keep up. Then, when you hit a running walk (a four-beat gait timed left front/right rear/right front/left rear) your friend must go into a rough, bone-jarring trot.

Walkers are also known for a rocking-chair canter, in case you ever get tired of the running walk. They're renowned for their gentle disposition and kindly nature. They want to go, but their spirit is not explosive and unpredictable. Most are good-sized horses, perhaps a tad taller than the average quarter horse, but somewhat lighter in body. They come in all colors—black is the show favorite—but colorful roans are coming back into vogue now. Incidentally, all horses pictured in this book are Tennessee walking horses.

Most of what I've said about Tennessee walking horses applies also to their cousins, the Missouri foxtrotters. These, too, have roots in the all-purpose, smooth-gaited horses of the American South. As a formalized breed with an official registry, foxtrotters are newer than walkers, and their registry was closed somewhat later. Thus, many foxtrotter registration papers contain the names of great stallions of the walking horse breed. The foxtrot is a wonderful gait, similar to the running walk, but reversed in timing (right rear/left front/left rear/right front) and without the walker's pronounced head nod. But such distinctions are tricky because of the overlap between the two breeds. I've seen many foxtrotters that prefer a running walk, and I've seen several walkers that fox-trot.

Like the Tennessee walker, the Missouri foxtrotter has gained a considerable following in the Rocky Mountain region. The U.S. Forest Service uses them in many areas.

The Peruvian paso, Columbian paso, and paso fino are tough, smooth-gaited breeds from Central and South America. All have fast, four-beat gaits, and all are known for their toughness. The Peruvian and Columbian pasos have a saddle gait similar to the running walk, with the addition of "termino," a throwing-out of the front feet to the side to make way for the long-stepping rear feet. (Tennessee walkers also overstride to a great degree—that's what makes even their flat-footed walk so much faster than a conventional walk—but their hind feet come up just after the front ones get out of the way.) The paso fino steps off with blazing speed and extremely short steps.

These are interesting, energetic breeds, smaller on average than walkers or foxtrotters, but strong and capable of carrying great loads. Because their registries in the U.S. are still small, these horses tend to be expensive, but that situation should gradually change. If I have a criticism of these breeds for backcountry use, it's that I see so few with a really effective flat-footed walk—and that's the most common gait when leading pack animals through rough country.

The American saddle horse, nicknamed "American saddler" and "gaited horse," is the prince of American breeds. Regal in appearance with a slim, arched neck, the saddlebred exudes style and refinement. An all-American breed, saddlebred stallions contributed greatly to the Tennessee walking horse, both by common ancestry and, later, by the genes of a stallion named Giovanni. Many early saddlebreds had natural four-beat gaits, and even in a trot the breed tends to be smoother than many others. Their long pasterns make them look as if they're propelled on shock absorbers.

Today the breed is thought of by many as a show horse. Certainly they are magnificent whether shown in the three-gait or five-gait class. Their rack (left rear/left front/ right-rear/right-front) stepped off with machine-gun rapidity is wonderful both to watch and to feel as a rider. But the saddlebred is an all-around performer, too. A rancher painted me a vivid word picture of a man riding a sorrel saddlebred with blaze and socks, followed by five more exactly like it carrying packs. The party was walking fast, their socks flashing in the sun, coming out of the mountains at the end of the pack trip. The rancher, though a quarter horse man, couldn't help but admire the sight, and he saved the picture in his mind.

The Morgan horse is another all-American that's been recognized as a distinct breed since a remarkable stallion named Justin Morgan began to acquire fame and fortune by throwing colts exactly like himself—small, solid, versatile animals that could pull a buggy or carry a rider or compete in a sprint race, all with equal aplomb. (Actually, the stallion's name was Figure, but he was later given the name of the man who owned him.) To many horse folks, Morgan means versatile. Traditionally, the horses were shorter and rounder than saddlebreds or walkers, with muscular necks.

Morgans are so useful that their blood has been sought to cross with many other strains. In my part of the West, Morgan studs were used by the Army Remount Service and also by farmers to cross with their work mares. This yielded work horses that were slightly smaller and more athletic than their mothers but still large enough to pull anything that needed pulling. Today, as in many breeds, the Morgan faces some division within its association. Some folks are devoted to the old-time horse; others prefer a more refined, lighter-built version. I saw a beautiful young stallion of the latter type once and honestly thought I was looking at a saddlebred. In any case, backcountry horse people should not overlook Morgans as a breed. It's extremely well suited to mountain and family use.

The American quarter horse has won the popularity poll by such astounding numbers that there are more registered quarter horses in America than there are registrations for all other breeds combined! This is strong testimony to both the animal and to its human backers. Although rare in the West before 1940, to many, the quarter horse is the horse of the West. Their early American roots grew from the muscular horses that sprinted well in quarter-mile races—thus the name—but the breed formalized largely through the efforts of the King ranch in Texas, which crossed Thoroughbred stallions with native cow-pony mares.

Today, quarterhorses fall under two major classifications: the traditional, muscular, wide-chested type (in extreme form called the "bulldog" type); and the running quarter horse, an animal with a higher percentage of Thoroughbred blood. The traditional type has been bred as stock horses and arena athletes. Their heavy muscling and wide build make for great acceleration and ability to move laterally, both important in cutting. Those same attributes do not indicate endurance or smoothness of ride. The running type is likely to be higher-withered and a bit taller and leggier. Being the slightest bit critical of such an incredibly popular breed has its hazards, but here goes. Within some strains of quarter horse, athletic ability in the short haul has been bred in place of endurance, and smoothness of gait is irrelevant. Worse, the walk, the most important backcountry gait, has been so underemphasized that some quarter horses cannot walk as fast as an active human without breaking into an annoying little dog trot. Another problem has been breeding the feet out from under the animal—developing strains with cute, tiny feet; that's fine, until you remember that since the days of ancient Greece, horsemen have understood the foot *is* the horse. Mount a muscular 1,200-pound animal on tiny feet (double or triple 0 size) and you have tremendous potential for failure. My cowboy farrier is blunt about this: He says when he is called out to shoe such a horse, he has few hopes his job with that animal will last many years. He says, "By the time they'd be eight or nine, those horses just aren't around anymore."

My last criticism is a matter of style. I consider big pads on the feet of "big lick" Tennessee walkers to be artificial and ugly, and I feel the same way about the "down-in-the-dirt" head carriage trained into many quarter horses. This ridiculous stance, which makes the horse appear to slope like an inclined plane down from rump to head, has no functional use. Horses absolutely can not see the trail better with their heads down in it. (Close in front of their faces, horses have a blind spot, and a little further out they see double, according to some.) If they could handle rough country better with their noses on deck, we should see wild horses, who live in the roughest country of all, with a similar head carriage. True, a trail horse should not throw his head to the sky; but why judges continue to select horses that walk two miles per hour with drooping heads as winners in pleasure classes is beyond me. Riding such a creature is not my idea of pleasure.

All this is not intended to indict, at large, one of the world's great breeds of horses. Within this most popular of the world 's breeds are tens of thousands of wonderful, athletic horses. But with all breeds, we must watch for negative trends, and we should not assume a breed's popularity guarantees its suitability for all things.

The Arabian horse is such a creature of legend it defies characterization in few words. But, trusting that readers interested in any of the breeds I'm touching upon in this appendix will do additional serious, in-depth reading beyond this, I'll try to give a quick distillation. The Arab can be thought of as the world's great foundation breed. Virtually all light horse breeds have been enlivened, at one time or another, with Arab blood. Certainly Arabians are the oldest continually recognizable breed, bred by people who idolized their horses for several thousand years. The characteristic head of the Arabian horse, often with dished face, is still the calendar-maker's favorite, and the horse is often sought for its beauty alone. Many a millionaire, with little interest in interaction with horses, has bought an Arab stallion simply to look at, to have on his estate as a thing of beauty.

As workers, Arabs can do most anything, but they are best known today as endurance champions. Although other breeds do well, the Arabians continually dominate endurance competition. Their build is narrow and refined, deep in the chest, and short-backed. There are no superfluous muscles—all are functional. As family and backcountry horses, Arabians are certainly viable, but their reputation for hot-bloodedness tends to make many consider them animals for accomplished horsemen and horsewomen.

The Appaloosa is a western breed known for its spots, which may cover the entire body or appear only on the rump "blanket." Tracing its heritage to horses raised by the Nez Perce Indians in Idaho, this breed is an interesting and popular one. As with all the breeds discussed here, considerable variety of type exists, and some owners who race horses have introduced Thoroughbred blood to the line. The Appaloosas in my vicinity tend more to the stock-horse type, some with the sparse manes and tails found in some individuals of the breed.

Another popular breed is the paint. Perhaps it's an oversimplification, but I see the paint as a breed for those who like quarter and running-quarter conformation but with a splash of color. The greatest impetus for growth of this breed may well be the exclusion from registration, in the largest quarter horse association, of any animal having white above the knees. The American Paint Horse Association accepts animals with certain color characteristics of registered quarter horse or Thoroughbred background, and this has provided a home for many excellent horses whose only crime was being born with too much "chrome."

Without pretending to have covered all the many breeds available (I haven't touched the world's greatest sport horse, the Thoroughbred), I'll turn briefly to ponies. Earlier in this book I intimated my affection for these creatures.

In the United States "pony" is most likely to mean one of two breeds, the Shetland or the Welsh, or crossbreeds resulting from breeding a full-sized horse to one of these. Both originated in extremely harsh sections of the British Isles, both subsist on meager feed, have tough feet, and are long-lived. Both come in several size classifications in their breeds. In the United States, Welsh ponies average a bit larger than Shetlands and often look like little, stocky Arabs. We owned two delightful Welsh mares and for several years raised American walking ponies (walker/Welsh cross) from them.

If any creature doesn't know it is little, it's a Welsh pony. Never intimidated by larger horses, Welsh ponies are athletic go-getters that can perform work all out of proportion to size. With tough feet that rarely need shoes, and a giant's attitude, a good Welsh pony would get my vote as the ultimate companion for the backpacker who wanted to take an entire family on long outings and needed a stalwart helper. With some of the advantages of the llama (smaller feed requirement and less environmental impact than a full-sized horse), a Welsh pony weighing 500-600 pounds is not only less expensive than a llama, it has many advantages. Compatible with other horses on the trail and stout enough to carry an adult if the need should arise, such a pony will stay in good condition on little feed expense the rest of the year and, if well trained, will entertain the kids in a lot healthier fashion than Nintendo. Even now that I've become a confirmed horse packer, the simplicity of a hiking trip in company with a Welsh helper (like Heather, a mare we used to own) has an awfully powerful appeal. I just may do it some day.

There are other pony breeds, of course. A rare and expensive but wonderful one is the Icelandic pony. Large enough to carry an adult with ease, the Icelandic has a gait called the tölt, a very fast form of running walk in which this pony can fly over the roughest terrain. As its numbers increase in the United States, and as its attributes become better known, this breed should explode in popularity.

Whatever breed strikes your fancy, do remember that breed identification doesn't make a horse. All the breeds contain champions as well as individuals riddled with faults. Nor should we neglect the grade horse, the just-plain horse, the non-registered animal that may be a jewel. It's a big equine world out there, and it's an arena where variety truly is the spice of life.

Appendix E:
Basic Knots for Packers

Knots are an integral part of a packer's knowledge. They are the "glue" that holds the packs together. Knowing how to tie these basic knots does not on its own guarantee a smooth trip, but not knowing how to properly secure your load essentially guarantees trouble on the trail. Practice until tying good knots becomes second nature.

The square knot.

The picket line loop (see Chapter Four).

The bowline, the only safe knot with which to tie a loop around an animal's neck.

1.

2.

An easy, quick-release tie-up knot. The end is passed through the loop as a last step to guard against the Houdini horse.

3.

4.

127

Appendix F: Tips on Horse Equipment and Its Use

The subject of tack for horses—or saddlery, as the British term it—is vast. Couple it with proper use of the equipment with which we harness animals to do our bidding, and you have material requiring many books and a lifetime of firsthand experience to master. This appendix replaces neither, but it offers some tips on riding gear and its proper use and on the choices that work best for the backcountry.

Even the smallest horse, even ponies, donkeys, and llamas, are incredibly strong compared to human beings—a seemingly obvious fact that some people can't assimilate. Respect for their strength is an absolute prerequisite for safety around large animals. It is also because of this strength that the halter is the standard means of control for equines and most other large domestic animals.

The poll area of a horse—the spot on top of the neck, just behind the ears—is extremely sensitive and is linked to the animal's central nervous system. Pull on a halter, and the strap passing over the poll exerts pressure on that spot. A "halter broke" horse has learned to give to any such pressure and do what the human boss wishes. In fact, the essence of all horse training is teaching the animal, with methods gentle but firm, to give to pressure. A stout halter is thus the first piece of equipment required for handling any of the large animals used for backcountry travel.

There are many good halters: some are made of heavy nylon strapping; more traditional ones are made from cotton rope—not as strong, perhaps, but less likely to chafe the horse. Growing in popularity are halters made of super-strength synthetic rope and assembled with no hardware whatsoever, just cleverly tied, adjustable knots. These halters are virtually unbreakable, since it is invariably the hardware in a halter that fails.

When haltering an animal always approach from the side toward the shoulder, not from either directly back or front. I once sold an extremely gentle mare to a man who turned out to be less experienced than I judged. He stopped by to say he liked the mare, but she was hard to catch, and she had taken to throwing her head up when he came toward her with the halter. I was mystified. As we talked we noticed that my gentle stallion, Trapper, in the corral on which we were leaning, had rubbed off his halter. My guest noticed this, climbed over the fence, picked up the halter, and walked toward the stallion. Having visited when the stallion was loose in a pasture with mares, the man, who had petted the horse lavishly at that time, thought he knew Trapper well enough to put his halter back on. I watched, a little horrified, as the man approached the horse directly from the front, holding the halter high in both hands. Even gentle Trapper shied away. The mystery was solved.

Horses fear things approaching from on high, probably a throwback to the days when cats jumped on them from out of trees. Further, their vision is nearly bilateral—one eye sees to one side, the other to the other side, and both function together only when they look toward the front or rear. Horses have a blind spot in their vision directly ahead, and they fear what they cannot see. (There is even evidence horses see double when looking at objects close to the front.) These facts make some show trail classes sponsored by the quarter horse folks, which require entries to walk with their noses practically in the dust, ridiculous—a horse can't study the footing as well from that range as he can from a natural, higher head carriage.

Thus, the safest approach is toward the shoulder both because the horse feels less threatened and because you're approaching

A halter without hardware, the most unbreakable kind.

A bullsnap in an eyesplice, best for a lead rope, but not infallible.

the part that has no weapons—rear feet that could kick back, or front feet that could strike. When the horse lets you, touch it on the shoulder. This confirms that you're there and friendly. Talk softly, with a firm tone.

The easiest way to halter a horse is to unbuckle the top strap that goes over the poll and secure the end of that strap firmly between the thumb and palm of your right hand. Hold the rest of the halter, wadded up, with your other fingers. Standing by the horse's left shoulder (American horses are traditionally trained more from the left or "near" side), slide your right hand, halter and all, up the shoulder of the horse and over its neck. Once your arm is over the neck, drop the halter, keeping your hold on only the end of the poll strap. Now it's a simple matter to reach under the neck and grasp the bottom of the halter with your left hand. At this point you

A ring snaffle bit.

A "Tom Thumb" bit.

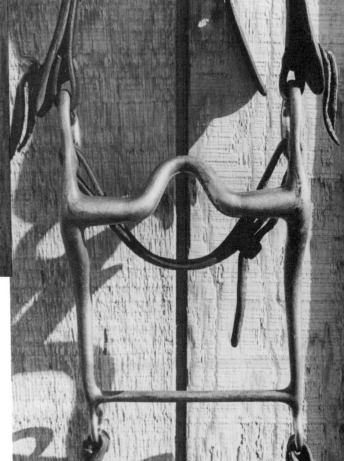

A typical curb bit.

have the horse (if it is trained). Now slide your right hand up the neck, giving slack, and place the nose portion of the halter over the horse's muzzle, rebuckle the halter, and it is done.

Always tie a horse with the halter and a good stout lead rope. Reins are for riding, lead ropes for tying . Forget all the old cowboy movies in which the reins are casually wrapped around the hitching rail in front of the saloon where the cowboy intends to spend a few hours. It just wasn't done that way—unless the cowboy intended to walk home. The safest tie is high (about head height) to something stout with a good quick-release knot. Since the halter and lead rope are the proper tools for the job, most mountain riding is done with the halter in place under the bridle. The lead rope can either be secured in place with a bowline around the horse's neck, just forward of the saddle, or to the saddle. I like to run a loop of it up through the gullet (the open space under the front, or pommel, of the saddle), back up behind the horn, and looped over it. Or, you can remove the lead rope, coil it, and tie it on to the saddle strings or with the lariat strap.

The lead rope itself should have a heavy snap (bullsnap) with swivel on one end and a backsplice on the other. The backsplice is preferable to a knot for preventing the end from sliding through your hand in a pull-back situation. Actually, it's better yet to eliminate the snap completely and simply splice an eye (loop) into one end. Pass the loop through the halter ring, then the end of your lead rope through the loop, and pull tight. It takes a couple seconds longer to attach this way than with a snap, but the usual source of breakage (the snap) is eliminated and the lead rope is lighter and quieter.

By the way, horses that truly learn to pull back are usually ruined for tying for life. Such a horse can never be trusted again, and many will pull so hard that they'll injure themselves. Usually the only way to hold a true puller is with an extremely strong rope tied with a bowline (the only safe knot for the purpose) around the neck, the other end tied to something extremely strong. Tragically, pullers are made, not born. They are made because some fool ties them with inadequate equipment (reins, or a weak halter or lead rope), something frightens them, they pull back and discover they can break loose. The truly determined types never forget that, and they challenge each restraint tried on them. My first mare, Rosie, a quarter horse-Thoroughbred cross, had been spoiled this way and was impossible to tie. Although a nylon rope and bowline could hold her, she would pull so terribly that we were afraid she would injure herself. Besides, there were few posts on the ranch strong enough to hold her. My "solution" was to pack hobbles wherever I went and hobble her while I did my work, watching that she didn't stray too far.

The next tool for horse control is, of course, the bridle. Hackamores are bitless bridles that rely on several types of mechanical pressure for control. Although I have a passing familiarity with them, I do not use them personally and recommend that you rely on other sources for instruction on them. I'm devoted to single-bitted, single-reined western riding, and the bit you are most likely to encounter on horses trained in this tradition is the curb bit. The curb comes in myriad configurations, but all have shanks to which the reins are attached, and usually the mouthpiece has a curved portion that lies on the tongue. Such a bridle exerts considerable leverage and must always be used gently. It exerts pressure on the bars of the mouth (the toothless portion between front and rear teeth), on the poll, and on the curb strap or chain that passes under the horse's mouth.

Before progressing to the curb bit, many horses are trained first on a snaffle—a shankless bit normally jointed in the center. With it, they become accustomed to the feel of a bit in their mouths, and they begin responding to direct-pressure reining. They may later progress to a bit that looks like a snaffle but with short shanks attached. (Any bit with shanks is technically a curb, though some call these "short-shanked snaffles"; in my region these are called Tom Thumbs.) Some horses work so well with these bits that a full-fledged curb is never required, but usually the curb is the "mature" bit.

Horses in the Rocky Mountains are always trained to neck rein. The reins are held together in one hand, and the rider moves both gently together in the direction he or she wants the horse to turn. Neither rein is pulled. The horse feels the pressure of a rein on the left side of his neck, for instance, and moves away from it, toward the right. This tradition of riding evolved to leave one hand free to swing a lariat or whip, to handle a rifle, or to lead a packhorse. To do most of the tasks I personally perform on horseback, being hampered by the necessity of holding one rein in each hand, English style, would be inconceivable.

Saddles exist to give riders a more secure seat than sitting directly on the horse's back. All saddles consist of a framework called a "tree," traditionally of wood and rawhide but sometimes now of plastic, covered, usually, with leather. Historians think the course of history changed drastically when one prominent feature of the saddle, the stirrup, was invented. The groups which thought of it first soundly trounced their enemies in battle, for the stirrup provided riders with the leverage and security necessary to effectively wield heavy weapons from horseback. Like riding styles, saddles vary with geogra-

Contrasting saddles. Emily's Connolly Brothers stock saddle purchased new by her father in 1919, and a flat English saddle. Both have their uses, but packing with the English saddle would be difficult—there's no way of tying anything on!

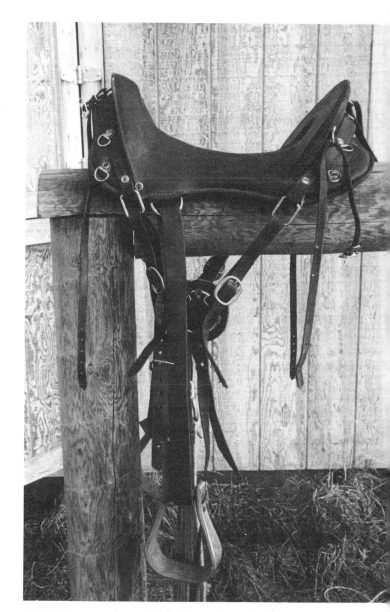

A McClellan cavalry saddle replica. Many find the seat comfortable, and ours works well as a spare pack saddle.

...try use is heavy ... or work rather ... are most suit-... lderness saddle ... things on—it ... D-rings strate-

...ar English "flat" ...ortable and per- ... the trail for an ...itional western ...tern wilderness ...ecause it is rug-...ugh sometimes ...s useful in many ...ich it was origi-...pack horse with ...l the horn, and ...f the pack horse ...ing. Most west-...umber of saddle ... gear, and most ...e to distribute ...rse.

...l, if you're trav-...s discussed in ...r saddle types are outstanding. The field trial saddle from the South has most of the attributes of the western saddle and is extremely comfortable. Most have an ample number of D-rings to which one can tie things. The Australian stock saddle is popular too, though expensive. Models made in Asia, rather than Australia, cost less than half as much, but I have no knowledge of their quality. Perhaps to satisfy western Americans, the Australians are now pushing models with horns. Australian saddles normally have "bucking rolls" contoured into the front of the seat itself rather than into the pommel. At first glance these have an added-on look, but in practice most riders find the saddles extremely comfortable. Like field trial saddles, most Australian saddles have D-rings rather than saddle strings.

McClellan saddles were the standard for the U.S. Cavalry from after the Civil War until World War II, and many of the originals are still serviceable. They are quite popular, too, and many find them comfortable. I own a replica built on a fiberglass tree. Its shape is comfortable, but its seat is extremely hard. I have trouble locating the stirrup buckle so that it doesn't gall my leg. (I think that's why cavalrymen wore such godawful high boots.) If you get along with

133

them, however, as many do, the McClellan is a good backcountry saddle.

Whatever the type, your saddle should fit your horse, and if you are not confident judging this, get some help. My wife and I ride in the saddles left us by her parents, early western stock saddles. Emily's was made in 1919. These fit our Tennessee walking horses extremely well, for western horses at that time were built like our walkers—high withered and narrow-to-moderate in width. In the early 1950s the "bulldog" quarter horse became very popular out west, and the "quarter horse tree" was developed for saddles that would be used on this broader horse. Such saddles can be used on narrower, high-withered horses only if you put an extra pad or two underneath; otherwise, the horse's withers are likely to contact the saddle in the gullet, underneath the pommel, and that's bad business.

Under the saddle you must put a pad. Originally, wool blankets made for the purpose and folded double were standard, and they're still excellent. Western saddles came with some built-in padding underneath, usually sheepskin with the fleece side exposed, so additional thick padding under the saddle was not considered necessary. Today many excellent pads are available, and the better ones probably offer the horse's back more protection than blankets. Place the pad forward of its natural position when you lay it on the back of the horse; then, slide it back to lay the hair down naturally under the pad.

Onto this pad you swing the saddle, with the off-side (right) stirrup and cinch pulled over the top toward you so they won't get caught under the saddle. Western saddles are either double or single rigged. Single rigged ones have just one cinch. Double rigged saddles have two cinches, the front one designed to do virtually all the holding, the rear intended to be just snugged. Its purpose is to prevent the rear of the saddle from rising when forward pull (from a calf or steer) is put on the horn during roping. *It is impor-tant to always attach the front cinch first and take it off last!* Never deviate. Never allow a saddle to be partially attached to the horse. Cinch up the front (holding cinch), then go ahead with the rear and then the breast collar. Reverse the procedure when unsaddling. Even the gentlest horse can be frightened into a blowup. Maybe a bee will sting it or some other unscheduled horror will occur. If only the rear cinch is in place when that happens, the saddle is going to rotate under the horse's belly and your thousand-dollar pride and joy is going to be fit for the garbage disposal by the time Dobbin gets done with it.

Breast collars help prevent your saddle from sliding backward when climbing. Particularly if your horse has a svelte figure (small belly), this is an important function. Further, on a horse with poor withers or a sausage-shaped barrel, a breast collar helps resist the saddle's rotation when you step in the stirrup to mount. If you're leading a pack string or intend to drag in firewood logs with a dally around the horn, a breast collar is essential. I like heavily built leather ones, though the fleece-lined nylon types are good, too. Watch the adjustment of any type you use, however. Some have metal rings in the center and/or on sides, and these can quickly gall a horse if the collar is adjusted too tightly.

On the reverse end are devices used to prevent the saddle from slipping forward. The best "device," of course, is a good set of withers on the anatomy of the saddle horse. Good withers make it impossible for the saddle to slip forward and, literally, go over the neck and off the front end when descending a steep grade. Such horrors have happened. If you must ride a horse with poor withers (several of the breed associations took to breeding animals designed to travel only in trailers and perform only in arenas, so some such horses exist), you can remedy the situation with a crupper or a breeching ("britchin'"). The crupper is simply a strap back from the saddle which circles the base of the tail. A horse's tail is a strong limb, and the animal will learn to tuck it down tightly on downgrades, holding back the saddle. A breeching, borrowed from a pack saddle or harness, will perform the same function even more admirably. Mules, by the way, rarely have prominent withers, so if a saddle mule is your animal of choice, you'll need either a crupper or a breeching.

When it comes to the whole subject of horses, horsemanship, and the gear necessary to make it work, it's good to proceed with the same caution you adapt when learning to gather mushrooms in the wild. You don't simply buy a book or two and then go out and try everything. With mushrooms, you learn, absolutely learn, one species at a time. When you know beyond a shadow of a doubt how to positively identify that species, you can pick it and eat it, and then move on to another.

If you want to get into the backcountry with horses, it's not necessary to learn everything at once. Buy several books, join a saddle club, talk to experienced people, immerse yourself in equines, and concentrate on gaining thorough knowledge one step at a time. Don't overlook the little things, things experienced horse people often mistakenly assume everyone knows, so they don't bother to tell you or write about them. For example, never lead a horse or other large animal by wrapping the lead rope around your hand. It's okay to double the rope a time or two making it thicker and providing a better handle, and it's okay to hold onto the rope with both hands. But to wrap it around a hand is to create a potentially dangerous situation in case of a major spook, a possible wreck in which you could be pulled down and dragged. Cautions like this are simple indeed, but very important.

Learn the basics, how to saddle and bridle, how to pick up feet, how to tie a bowline and square knot, and how to ride using your body, not just the reins. All this will come in time. Meanwhile, don't miss out on the experience simply because you don't feel competent yet. Go with someone. If you can afford it, take an outfitted trip. Consider the hands-on horsepacking schools and clinics advertised today in major horse publications. Go along with a more experienced friend, pitching in on the work side of it, for it's there that you'll learn.

But do it. There are few experiences in this life that equal the joy of riding a fast-walking horse in mountain country, perhaps with a pack horse on your lead rope. As you smell the pine breeze sifting down the canyon and through the trees, there is the sense that you are your own little survival unit, ready for anything.

1. Travel as lightly as possible, within your party's limits of comfort and safety. If backpacking with a pack dog, this takes care of itself—you'll soon learn to leave unnecessary items behind. If combining horse packing with backpacking, one horse should be adequate for a family, but it may take two llamas and either one or two ponies. Traveling mounted with horses or mules, one pack horse per two people should be maximum. We can usually get the ratio up to two pack horses for five people or one pack horse to three people. Remember, the fewer animals the less impact.

Assemble your camp equipment with lightness and compactness constantly in mind. Often backpacking equipment can be substituted for traditional horse packing gear. Modern materials have lightened some traditional items, such as wall tent models that now weigh about half as much as similar tents in traditional heavy weaves of canvas.

2. Pack out all garbage or, indeed, anything you pack in. Do not bury trash. Burn things truly burnable where legal, but keep foil wrappers and other non-burnables out of the firepit. Pick up trash left by other parties as well. End your stay with a thorough, on-line "policing" of the area.

3. Build (where legal) only campfires that follow low-impact methods. Do not use rocks to retain the fire. Remove the sod in a circle, put it aside intact, then, when done, scatter cold ashes and replace the sod, topping it off with a little water to get the grass growing again. Better yet, if space allows, consider taking along a steel fire platform or a galvanized metal oil drain pan, and line your firepit with that. Commercially made "fire blankets" should be available soon, if not already; they are the latest in new technology. Whatever the method, never leave your campfire unattended.

4. Use only down, dead wood for firewood.

5. Cook over stoves rather than campfires. True, both methods burn fossil fuels, but the stove is vastly more efficient and doesn't generate smoke. Depending on the location and the fire danger (as rated by the Forest Service), campfires may not be legal.

6. Do not cut any living trees or shrubs—use a pad or air mattress, not pine boughs, for your bed.

7. Bury human waste in single holes a shovel-blade deep; replace the sod to make the area look as it did when you found it. Treat dog waste the same way. Select sites on high ground, at least 200 feet from streams, lakes, or places that drain toward them during wet seasons of the year. Use only white, unscented toilet paper, and bury that with the waste.

8. Keep livestock out of the camp area itself. If camping with horses, mules, or llamas, bypass campsites better suited to backpackers. If the rainy season is in progress and the weather has been wet, consider postponing your trip. Animal feet (and those of humans) do more damage when the ground is wet, and leaving muddy bogs, laden with the tracks of your pack animals—besides scarring the countryside—hurts all of our reputations in the eyes of those who oppose pack animals.

9. Keep all livestock at least 100 feet from streams and lakes. Take them to water in a rocky place twice each day rather than leaving them to water themselves.

10. Hobble stock rather than picketing when possible. Tie to trees only when there is no option, and then only to large ones for extremely short duration; for long-term tying use a high picket line stretched between two trees with a dutchman or other system with mechanical advantage and with tree-savers, cinches, or wide straps around the trees. Select a rocky site for this, and move whenever possible. Use an electric corral, which can be moved often, in preference to the high picket line when possible.

If you do picket stock out to graze, move often so that grazed rings do not result. Again, consider the electric corral, but check to make sure grazing is legal.

11. Any dogs brought along should be in a working (packing) capacity, and a chain should be brought for restraint in camp. Do not allow your pack dog to visit the camps of others or to bother others on the trail.

12. In camp, do not drive nails into trees.

13. Do not trench your tent.

14. When traveling, stay on the trail. Don't cut switchbacks. Respect Forest Service efforts to "steer" your path around badly eroded stretches of trail by placing obstacles over them.

15. When leaving a campsite, tend not just to your fire but to the entire area. Leave nothing. Scatter horse or mule droppings.

16. If you smoke, be ultracareful with the fire. (Better yet, use your outdoor trip and its change of surroundings to quit.) Never leave a cigarette butt behind. The filter, especially, is not biodegradable. Adopt the habits that have been enforced on military smokers for years: completely extinguish the cigarette, then put it in your pocket. Later, that night, burn it in the campfire or pack it out.

17. Do not overgraze fragile areas. Unless you're certain there will be abundant natural feed for your livestock, pack plenty in. Certified weed-free hay is best. Pellets or grain should be fed in containers to minimize spillage and possible distribution of weed seeds. (Certified weed-free pellets are available in some areas.)

18. Be certain your dogs, llamas, ponies, horses, or mules do not transmit unwanted weeds to the backcountry. Clean their coats thoroughly before leaving home. Start them on weed-free feed a couple of days before the trip so unwanted seeds aren't transplanted by their manure.

19. Treat the outdoors as if it were your livingroom. You may not like picking up after others, but if boorish guests visited your house, you'd do so after they left. Similarly, pick up and pack out the trash left by others. If we all pitch in, the backcountry will not be littered, and most of the slobs will eventually learn.

Index

fire platform, 54
first-aid kit, 46, 82, 115, 116, 118
flat-footed walk, 121
flight plan, 46
fly spray, 116
folding canvas bucket, 116
folding saw, 116
Fort Peck Reservoir, 75
fox-trot, 120
freeze-dried foods, 117
Frisbee, 79
Frostline kits, 3

gaited breeds (of horses), 41, 120
Galiceno pony, 120
generators (for Coleman products), 117
German shepherd, as pack dog, 7
Giardia, 54
Giovanni, 122
goat, as pack animal, 13
goose down, 66
gooseneck trailer, 94
Gore-tex, 65
gorp, 80
graze rope, 41

hackamore, 131
half-breed (on Decker), 20, 100
haltering, method of, 129
Hemingway, Ernest, 47
high picket line, 57-59
hip dysplasia, 7
hobbles, 41, 47
hobbling, 56
Hollowfill II, 66
hoof pick, 116
Horse Packing in Pictures, 26
horse trailers, 92-94
Horses, Hitches, and Rocky Trails, 26
humane tree on sawbuck, 21, 28

Icelandic pony, 124
Indian reservations, 89
Indians, use of dogs, 4

King ranch, 122

Labrador retriever, as pack dog, 7
lantern, 116
leafy spurge, 61
leather repair kit, 116
llama, 11-13
loft (in sleeping bags), 67

Maglite flashlights, 71
manties, 18, 29-34, 36, 98
manure, 53
margarine, 117
McClellan saddle, 24, 133
meat, frozen, transport of, 117
milk, 81
Missouri foxtrotter, 41, 120, 121
Montana, 25, 39, 50, 100
Morgan horse, 120, 122
mountain bike, 104
Mountain Manners, 89, 113
MSR stove, 70
mule, 14
mule deer, 108
multiple-use lands, 88

national parks, 88
neck rein, 132
Nez Perce, 124
Nordic dog breeds, as pack dogs, 7

Optimus stoves, 70

pack goats, 115
Packin' In on Mules and Horses, 26-27
packing clinics, 22-23, 26
paint horse, 124
panniers, 28
paso fino, 121
Peruvian paso, 41, 121
picket line loops, 115
picketing, 41, 46, 56
pickup trucks (as tow vehicles), 91
plantation saddle, 41
pointers (as pack dogs), 7
Polarguard, 66
poll (on horse), 128
pony, as pack animal, 13
possibles, 44
private lands, 89
professional outfitters, 25-26

rack (gait), 122
Relite, 61, 64
retrievers, 7
Rocky Mountain Elk Foundation, 64
Rocky Mountain Pack Goats, 13
Rollatable, 71, 104
running walk, 120, 121

saddle packs, 43
saddle pad, 134